THE DANISH WAY OF PARENTING

JESSICA ALEXANDER &
IBEN DISSING SANDAHL MPF

FORLAGET
EHRHORN HUMMERSTON

© 2014 Forlaget Ehrhorn Hummerston,
Copenhagen

Printed in Denmark
ISBN 978-87-92559-31-9
1st edition, 1st printing

Design and layout: Ehrhorn Hummerston
Illustrations: Joakim Wei Nørgaard

Fonts: Verlag, Calibri

Forlaget Ehrhorn Hummerston
Gråbrødretorv 6-8
DK 1154 Copenhagen K
www.forlaget-eh.dk

CONTENTS

PARENT

P
PLAY 25
Why free play creates happier, better adjusted, more resilient adults.

A
AUTHENTICITY 45
Why honesty creates a stronger sense of self. How praise can be used to form a growth mindset rather than a fixed mindset, making your children more resilient.

R
REFRAMING 65
Why reframing can change you and your children's lives for the better.

E
EMPATHY 87
Why understanding, incorporating and teaching empathy is fundamental in creating happier children and adults.

N
NO ULTIMATUMS 109
Why avoiding power struggles and using a more democratic parenting approach fosters trust, resilience and happier kids.

T
TOGETHERNESS AND HYGGE 133
Why a strong social network is one of the biggest factors in our overall happiness and by creating hygge (coziness) we can give this powerful gift to our children.

Special Thanks

JESSICA ALEXANDER

I'd like to thank my mom and dad for their unconditional love and for always believing in me. To my sister for her invaluable love and friendship. To my husband and his family for inspiring me to write *The Danish Way* in the first place. And to our two wonderful children, the guiding lights of our life.

And to Iben, who without her contribution and expertise, *The Danish Way* could not have come to fruition.

IBEN DISSING SANDAHL

First of all, I want to thank my husband for always supporting me and telling me that everything will work out fine. He has been a great help in the process of producing the book, and has had to put up with my absence.

And a special thanks to my two beautiful daughters—without them I would not be the person I am today. I also want to thank my mother and father, who gave me life and have always supported me.

I am fortunate to be surrounded by intelligent and interesting friends and colleagues who listen, ask good questions and inspire me.

And a special thanks to Jessica for being so brave as to take the initiative to write this book.

ABOUT THE BOOK

THE MAKING OF THE THEORY AND A DISCLAIMER

When my friends heard that I had co-written a parenting book, they all laughed. "You? The most non-maternal woman we know co-wrote a parenting book?" The irony is, it was precisely due to my lack of natural mothering skills that made me so interested in the Danish Way in the first place. It had changed my life so profoundly that I knew, if it could help me, it could definitely help others.

You see, I wasn't born with all of those innate nurturing mother skills supposedly all women are born with. I don't have a problem admitting it. I wasn't a kid person. I didn't even like kids that much if I am to be completely honest. I became a mom because that's what people do. So you can imagine my deep-seated fear when I got pregnant and thought "How in the world am I going to do this? Surely I am going to be a terrible mom!" And so I got busy reading every parenting book I could get my hands on. I read a lot. I learned a lot. But still, the fear remained.

To my good fortune, I was married to a Dane. For over 8 years I had been exposed to the Danish culture and one thing I noticed was that they were clearly doing something right with their children. Overall, I consistently observed happy, calm, well-behaved kids and I wondered what their secret was. But there was no parenting book I could find on the subject.

When I finally became a mother, I found myself doing the only natural thing for me, which was to ask my Danish friends and family for every single answer to every single question I had. From breastfeeding to disciplining to education, I preferred their off-the-cuff answers to all the books I had on my shelf! Through this journey, I discovered a philosophy of raising children that opened my eyes and changed my life completely.

My good friend Iben and I discussed the idea. Iben is a Danish psychotherapist with many years of experience working with families and children and together we asked the question "Does a Danish Way of parenting exist?" To her knowledge, it didn't. We looked high and low for some literature on the subject, but there was nothing. In all her years working in the Danish school system and being a family psychotherapist, she had never heard of "a Danish Way." She knew all the academic theories and the research on parenting practices she used daily, but could there be a valid parenting style embedded in her very own culture she hadn't seen?

The more we talked about it, the more it became clear that there was a Danish parenting philosophy but it was woven so tightly into the fabric of Denmark that it wasn't immediately visible to the Danish eye. The more we looked at it, the more the pattern emerged from the fabric. And there it was, laid out before us: The Danish Way of Parenting.

The Danish Way is our theory based on years of experience, research, supporting studies and facts about Denmark. Iben is an expert in her field and everything that is written is a "we", representing our beliefs and research compiled together. It is sometimes my voice, contributing with personal anecdotes, and sometimes quotes from Iben with her professional input as well as many supporting studies and cultural examples. We have both learned so much along this journey. The commentary on Denmark comes from research on the school system, government, parents, psychologists and teachers. The collaboration was wholly equal and all of the supporting studies can be found in the back of the book.

We would like to clarify that this is not a political statement nor is it a book about living in Denmark. It is a parenting theory, which we believe is one of the leading factors as to why the Danes are voted so consistently happy. Happy kids grow up to make happy adults who make happy kids and so on.

We also know that it is not the only reason why the Danes are happy. We know there are many reasons for their happiness and there are certainly unhappy people living there as well. Happiness can have many different meanings. We don't claim to be working off of one in particular. Denmark is not utopia and surely it has its own internal matters to deal with, as does every country. Nor is this book in any way meant to be disparaging to America. America is an enormous country and the facts we state in the book are generalizations. I, personally, am very proud to be American and I love my country dearly. I have merely had the coincidental opportunity to see the world with a very different pair of glasses on. A "Danish brand", if you will, and it has changed my whole perspective on life.

We would like to offer you these glasses to put on for yourself and see what you think when you look through them. When you look in the mirror at yourself as a parent and at the world around you in general, what do you think could be better?

If this book makes you open your eyes in any way and see even one thing differently, for us, it has been a success.

From "the most non-maternal person" to a happier parent and better human being, I can honestly say I have the Danish Way to thank for this change. We hope you will enjoy it.

What's the Secret to Their Happiness?

Denmark, a small country in the north of Europe famous for "The Little Mermaid", has been voted as having the happiest people in the world by the OECD (Organisation for Economic Co-operation and Development) for almost every single consecutive year since 1973. 1973! That's over 40 years of consistently being voted as the happiest people in the world! If you stop to think about that for a second, it's a staggering accomplishment. Even a new Happiness Report that was recently launched by the UN (United Nations) has seen Denmark top the list every single year since its inception. What is the secret to their satisfied success?

Countless articles and studies have been devoted to solving this mystery. Denmark? Why Denmark? 60 Minutes did a program on it—"The Pursuit of Happiness". Oprah did a show on it—"Why are the Danes so Happy?"—and the conclusions are always conveniently inconclusive. Is it the size of their social system, their houses or their government? It can't be the taxes or the weather, so what gives?

America, on the other hand, the country with "the pursuit of happiness" built into its very own Declaration of Independence isn't even in the top 10. It's barely in the top 20, closer to number 17 after Mexico. Despite having an entire field of psychology devoted to happiness and an endless sea of self-help books instructing us on how to acquire this elusive emotion, we aren't really that happy. Why is that? And, moreover, why are the Danes so content?

After 13 years of research, we think we have finally uncovered the secret as to why the Danes are so happy. And the answer, quite simply, is in their upbringing.

The Danish philosophy behind parenting and their way of raising children yield some pretty powerful results. Resilient, emotionally secure, happy kids who turn into the resilient, emotionally secure, happy adults who then repeat this powerful parenting style with their own kids. The legacy repeats itself and we get a society that tops the happiness charts for over 40 years in a row.

Through this amazing journey and discovery, we have decided to share this knowledge about "the Danish Way" of parenting with you. In this step-by-step guide, our goal is to help mothers and fathers who are about to embark on or who have already embarked on one of the most challenging and extraordinary jobs in the world. Incorporating this method takes practice, patience, resolve and awareness, but the outcome is well worth the work. Remember that this is your legacy. If your goal is to raise the happiest people in the world, then please read on. The real secret of the Danes' success is inside.

Countless articles and studies have been devoted to solving this mystery. Denmark? Why Denmark?

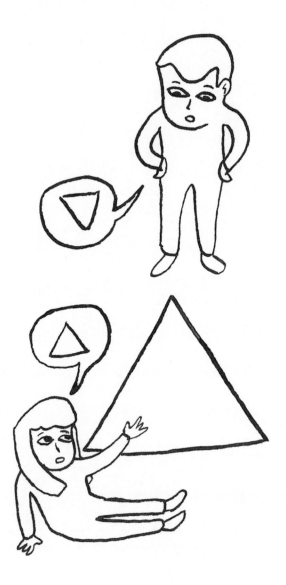

Cultural Differences and Paradigm Shifts

We have all thought from time to time about what it means to be a parent. Whether it be before the birth of your first child, during a toddler meltdown or during a fight at the dinner table over not eating their peas, we have all once thought "Am I doing this right?" Many of us refer to books and the Internet, or talk to friends and family for advice and support. Most of us just want to be reassured that we are, in fact, doing things the right way.

But have you ever considered what the right way is? Where do we get our ideas about the right way of parenting? If you go to Italy, you will see children eating dinner at 9pm and running around in restaurants until 11 or 12 at night, in Norway babies are regularly left outside in minus twenty degree weather to sleep and in Belgium kids are allowed to drink beer. To us, some of these behaviors seem bizarre but to these parents it is the "right way".

These implicit, taken-for-granted ideas we have about how to raise our children are what Sarah Harkness, a professor of human development at the University of Connecticut, calls "Parental Ethnotheories". She has studied this phenomenon for decades across cultures and what she has found is that these intrinsic beliefs about the right way to parent are so ingrained in our society that it's almost impossible to see them objectively. For us, it just seems to be the way things are.

And so, most of us have thought about what it means to be a parent but have you ever thought about what it means to be an American parent? About how the American glasses we wear correct our vision for seeing what "the right way" is?

What if we were to take those glasses off for a moment: what would we see? If we stood back and looked at America from a distance, what would our impression be?

For years we have seen a growing problem with people's happiness level across the board in America. Antidepressant use went up 400 percent between 2005 and 2008, according to the National Center for Health Statistics. Children are being diagnosed and prescribed medication for a growing number of psychological disorders, some with no clear-cut method of diagnosing them. In 2010 alone, there were at least 5.2 million children between the ages of 3-17 taking Ritalin for hyperactivity disorder.

We are fighting obesity, early onset of puberty or "precocious puberty" as it is now referred to. Girls and boys as young as seven and eight are getting injected with hormone shots to stop puberty. Most of us don't even question this as being strange but rather just the way things are. "My daughter is getting the shot," one mother rattled off nonchalantly the other day about her eight-year-old who she thought was hitting puberty too soon.

Many parents are excessively competitive with themselves, with their children and with other parents without even realizing it. Of course, not all people are like this, nor do they want to be, but they can also feel pressured living in this competitive culture and the language surrounding them. This language can be intense and challenging, putting people on the defensive: "Kim is just amazing at soccer. The coach says she is one of the best on the team. But she is still managing straight A's despite soccer, karate and swimming. I don't know how she does it! What about Olivia? How is she doing?" We feel pressure to perform, for our kids to perform, to do well in school and to fulfill our idea of what a successful kid should be, to fulfill our idea of what a successful parent should be. Stress levels are often high and we feel judged. We feel judged by others and by ourselves. We feel judged by our families and our friends and we judge others in turn. Part of this is human nature and part of this is what it is to be American. What is pushing us as a society to perform and compete and be successful to a standard that ultimately doesn't seem to be making us very happy as adults? What if some of the "answers" we have for raising our kids— our parental ethnotheories—are flawed?

What if we discovered that the glasses we were wearing had the wrong prescription in them and we weren't able to see things as clearly as we thought? So we change the lenses, fix the stigmatism and look again at our world. Lo and behold, things do look different! By trying to see things from a new perspective, with new lenses, the question arises naturally:

Is there a better way?
The Danish Way of Parenting is a guidebook aimed at charting a new path through the jungle of parenting. A better path. A path that leads to more resilient kids and happier adults. The results of this path have been seen for over 40 years in Denmark. This method has been developed through painstaking research and observation. It is our theory and we believe that it generally encompasses the philosophy of parenting in Denmark. Perhaps you will find some ideas you already have in practice and perhaps you will discover some you never even considered. The fact is, implementing even some of our tips from *The Danish Way* will guarantee positive changes not only in your children but also in your own self-esteem and satisfaction as a parent. It really does work!

Default Settings and Why They Need to Be Examined

The other day I was in the city with my almost three-year-old son. He was on a push-bike with no pedals and he started to push himself out towards the street despite me yelling at him numerous times to stop. I ran after him frantically, grabbing him hard by the arm and gave him a shake. I was furious and scared and was about to spank him on the bottom and yell, "You'd better stop when I tell you to stop!" I could see he was going to cry out of fear, and in that moment, it took all of my might to muster up the strength to go outside of myself and observe what I was doing. That wasn't how I wanted to react. I scanned my brain for another way and, miraculously, an answer was there. I stopped, took a breath and got down on his level. I held his arms in my hands and looked into his eyes imploringly. In a calm but concerned voice, I said, "Do you want to go ow ow? Mommy doesn't want you to go ow ow! Do you see those cars?" I pointed to the cars and he nodded. "Cars go ow ow to Sebastian!" He nodded, listening to me. "Cars. Ow ow." "So when mommy says to stop, you stop, ok? So that you don't go ow ow from the cars." He nodded. He didn't cry in the end. We hugged. I repeated what I had said and could feel him nodding on my shoulder. "Cars. Ow ow."

Five minutes later we were in the same situation. I told him to stop and he did. He stopped because he understood why I had told him to stop. He pointed to the road and shook his head. "Cars ow ow." I showed him how happy I was by jumping up and down and clapping. I wasn't just happy with him for stopping, you see. I was happy with myself for stopping. For stopping myself and changing my natural behavior, my default settings, in a difficult moment. It wasn't easy but doing this changed my output and the results made both of us happier for it.

Sometimes we forget that parenting, like love, is a verb. It takes effort and work to yield positive returns. There is an incredible amount of self-awareness involved in being a good parent. It requires us to look at what we do when we are tired and stressed and stretched to our limits. These actions are called our default settings. Our default settings are the actions and reactions we have when we are too tired to choose a better way.

Most of our default settings are inherited from our own parents. They are ingrained and programmed into us like a motherboard on a computer. They are the factory settings we return to when we are at our wit's end and not thinking and they have been installed into us from our upbringing. It's when we hear ourselves saying things we don't really want to be saying. It's when we act and react in ways we aren't sure we want to be acting and reacting. It's when we feel bad, because deep down we know there is a better way to get results from our kids but we aren't sure what it is. Anyone who has kids is familiar with this feeling.

That is why it is so important to look at your default settings and study them and understand them. What do you like about how you act and react with your children? What don't you like? What are you doing that is just a repeat from your own upbringing? What would you like to change? Only when you see what your natural inclinations as a parent are, your default settings, can you decide how you want to change them for the better.

The Danish Way is a guide to help you see what some of those positive changes can be. It gives clear and practical tips with the easy-to-remember acronymn PARENT—play, authenticity, reframing, empathy, no ultimatums and togetherness—to illustrate some of the tried-and-true methods that have been working for parents in Denmark for over 40 years.

If you manage to configure yourself with even some of these new settings, it will give you the option of having better output when you are under pressure. And this will change your life and your children's lives forever. These new settings will ensure that your reactions are based on thought and not just what you were programmed to think and do from your upbringing. Being aware of yourself and choosing your behavior is the first step towards powerful life change. This is how we become better people. This is how we become better parents. And this is how we leave a legacy of well-being in our wake to pass on to the next generations. Is there a greater gift you can give to your children and your children's children than to grow up to be happier, more secure and resilient adults? We don't think so.

Play

"Play is often talked about as if it were a relief from serious learning, but for children play is serious learning."

MR. ROGERS

Have you noticed that there is an unspoken or even spoken pressure to organize activities for your kids? Whether it is swimming, ballet, tee ball or soccer, somehow you just don't feel like you are doing your job if you don't have your kids signed up for at least 3 or 4 things a week. How many times do you hear parents saying that their Saturday is taken up with driving their children to various sports, lessons or activities?

When was the last time you heard someone say, "On Saturday, my daughter is going to play?"

And by play, we don't mean play the violin or play a sport or even go on a play date where adults have organized activities. We mean "play" where they are left to their own devices, with a friend or alone, to play exactly as they see fit for as long as they want. And even if parents do allow this free play to take place, there is often a niggling feeling of guilt admitting it. Because ultimately, we feel we are being better parents by teaching them something, having them involved in a sport or "giving" their little brains some input. Play, in a way, seems like a waste of valuable learning time. But is it?

In America in the last 50 years, the number of hours that a child was allowed to play has decreased dramatically. Aside from the television and technology, there is also our own fear of them getting hurt coupled with our desire to "develop" them, which has taken over much of the time they once had to play.

As parents, we feel comforted when our children are making visible signs of progress in something. We like watching them play soccer while others cheer them on or going to their ballet or piano recital. We feel proud to say that Billy won a medal or a trophy or learned a new song or can recite the alphabet in Spanish. It makes us feel like we are being good parents. We do it with the best intentions because by giving them more instruction and controlled activities, we are giving them training to become more successful, thriving adults. Or are we?

It's no secret that the number of anxiety disorders, depression and attention disorders have skyrocketed in America. Is it possible that we are making our kids anxious without realizing it by not allowing them to play more?

Are we overprogramming our kids' lives?

Many parents strive to start their children at school early or jump a grade. They learn to read and do math earlier and earlier and we are proud because they are "smart" and being smart or athletic are highly valued characteristics in our culture. We may go to great lengths with tutors and educational toys and programs to try to get them there. Success is success and these are tangible, visible, measurable signs. Free play, for all intents and purposes, seems fun but what is it really teaching them?

What if we told you that free play teaches children to be less anxious. It teaches them resilience. And resilience has been proven to be one of the biggest factors in predicting success as an adult! The ability to "bounce back", to regulate emotions and cope with stress are key factors in a healthy, functioning adult. We now know that resilience is great for preventing anxiety and depression and it's something the Danes have been instilling in their children for years. And one of the ways they have done it is by placing a lot of importance on play.

In Denmark, dating back to 1871, husband and wife Niels and Erna Juel Hansen came up with the first pedagogy based on educational theory, which incorporated play. They discovered that free play was crucial for a child's development. In fact, for many years, Danish children weren't even allowed to start school before they were seven. They didn't want them to engage in education because they felt that children should first and foremost be children and play. Even now, children up until the age of ten finish regular school at 2pm and then go to what is called "Skole/Fritidsordning" (free time school) for the rest of the day, where they are mainly encouraged to play. That is pretty incredible if you think about it.

In Denmark, there isn't a sole focus on education or sports but rather on the whole child. They focus on things like socialization, autonomy, cohesion, democracy and self-esteem. They want their children to learn resilience and develop a strong internal compass to guide them through life. They know their children will be well educated and learn many skills. But true happiness isn't coming only from a good education. A child who learns to cope with stress, makes friends, and yet is realistic about the world has a very different set of life skills than being a math genius, for example. And by life skills, the Danes are talking about all aspects of life. Not only career life. For what is a math genius without the ability to cope with life's ups and downs? All the Danish parents we spoke to said that excessive focus on "developing" children seemed very strange to them.

As they see it, if the children are always performing to obtain something—good grades, awards or praise from teachers or parents—then they don't get to develop their inner drive. They believe that children fundamentally need space and trust to allow them to master things by themselves, to make and solve their own problems. This creates real self-esteem because it comes from the child's own internal cheerleader, not someone else.

Internal vs. external locus of control

In psychology, this internal cheerleader or drive is known as the locus of control. A person's locus of control is used to describe the control a person believes they have over their own lives and the events that affect them. The word "locus" in Latin means "place" or "location" and so the locus of control is quite simply referring to the place from which one feels a sense of control over one's life. Thus, people with an internal locus of control believe that they have the power to control their lives and the events that happen around them. Their drive is internal or personal. Their place of control comes from the inside. People with an external locus of control believe that their lives are controlled by external factors like the environment or fate, which they have little influence over. What drives and controls them is coming from the outside and they can't change it. We are all affected by our surroundings, culture and social status, but how much we feel we can control our lives despite those factors is an internal versus external locus of control.

Studies have repeatedly shown that children, adolescents and adults who have a strong external locus of control (that is, that circumstances outside of themselves control their lives) are predisposed to anxiety and depression. When people believe they have little or no control over their fate, they become anxious, and when this sense of helplessness gets to be too great, they become depressed.

Research also shows that there has been a dramatic shift towards a more external locus of control among young people in the last 50 years. In studies conducted by psychologist Jean M. Twenge and colleagues, they examined results from a test called the Children's Nowicki-Stricklund Internal-External Control Scale (CNSIE) over a 50-year period. This test measures whether a person has an internal or an external locus of control. What they discovered was that there was a dramatic shift from an internal towards an external locus of control in children of all ages, from elementary school to college. To give you an idea of how great a shift it was, the average young person in 1960 was 80 percent more likely to claim that they had control over their lives than children in 2002, who were more prone to say they lacked personal control over their lives.

And what was even more striking was that the trend was more pronounced for elementary school children than for middle school and college kids. So younger and younger children were feeling the lack of control over their lives. They were feeling this sense of helplessness earlier and earlier. This rise in external locus of control over the years has a linear correlation with the rise in depression and anxiety in our society. What could be causing this shift?

Respecting the zone of proximal development

Much of Denmark's methodology is based on a concept called proximal development by Lev Vygotsky, a Russian developmental psychologist. This basically states that a child needs the right amount of space to learn and grow in the zones that are right for them with the right amount of help. Like helping a child climb over a fallen log in the forest. If at first they need a hand, you give the hand, but then perhaps only a finger to help them over and when it is time you let them go. You don't carry them over or push them over. In Denmark, parents try to intervene only when it is absolutely necessary. They trust their children to be able to do and try new things and give them space to build their own trust of themselves. They provide them with scaffolding for their development and help them build their self-esteem, and this is very important for the "whole child". If children feel too pressured, they can lose the joy in what they are doing and this can cause fear and anxiety. Instead, Danish parents try to meet children where they feel secure trying a new skill, and then challenge and invite them to go farther or try something new, while it still feels exciting and strange.

Giving this space and respecting the zone of proximal development allows a child to develop their internal locus of control because they feel they are in charge of their own challenges and development. A child who is pushed or pulled too much risks developing an external locus of control because they aren't controlling their development, rather external factors are and the foundation for their self-esteem becomes shaky.

We sometimes think we are helping kids by pushing them to perform or learn faster, but leading them at the right time in the right moment of their development will yield much better results. Not only because of the learning itself, which will surely be more pleasurable, but because the child will be more self assured of the mastery of their skills since they feel more in charge of acquiring them.

David Elkind, an American psychologist, agrees. Children who are pushed to read earlier, for example, may read better than their peers initially, but those levels even out in a few years' time and at what cost? The pushed children exhibit higher levels of anxiety and lower self-esteem in the long run.

Is it possible that we are making our kids anxious without realizing it by not allowing them to play more?

In America, we find an endless number of books on how to lower or reduce anxiety and stress. "No Stress", "Stop Stress Now", and so forth. We want to eliminate stress at all costs, particularly for our children. Many parents helicopter over their children and intervene to protect them at a moment's notice. Most of us barricade staircases and protect and lock up anything we can find that might be remotely dangerous. If we don't, we feel we are being bad parents and, in fact, we judge and are judged by others for not doing enough to protect them. These days require so many safeguarding gizmos and gadgets that one wonders how parents didn't kill their children 20 years ago.

Not only do we want to protect our children from stress but we also want to build their self-confidence and make them feel special. The standard method of doing this is to praise them, sometimes excessively, for insignificant accomplishments. But in our quest to increase confidence and reduce stress, we may actually be setting them up for more stress in the long run. Building confidence rather than self-esteem is like making a nice house with little foundation. We all know what happens when the big bad wolf comes.

But how, you may be wondering, can play help?
Scientists have been studying play in animals for years, trying to understand its evolutionary purpose. And one thing they are finding is that play is crucial for learning how to cope with stress. In studies done on domestic rats and rhesus monkeys, scientists found that when they were deprived of playmates during a critical stage of their development, these animals became "stressed out" as adults. They would overreact to stressful situations, unable to cope well in social settings. They would either react with excessive fear, sometimes running shaking into a corner, or with exaggerated aggression,

lashing out with rage. The lack of play was definitely the culprit, because when the animals were allowed a playmate for even an hour a day, they developed more normally and coped better as adults. It makes sense if you think about it.

Fight or flight behaviors, normally experienced in play, activate the same neurochemical pathways in the brain as stress does. Think about when you see dogs running around chasing each other for fun and growling. Many animals engage in this kind of play where they chase each other and put each other into the subordinate or attacker position in a play fight, creating a kind of stress. We know that exposing the brains of baby animals to stress changes them in a way that makes them less responsive to stress over time, meaning that the more they play the better their brains become at regulating stress as they grow. Their ability to cope constantly improves through playing and they are able to deal with more and more difficult situations. Resilience isn't cultivated by avoiding stress, you see, but learning how to tame and master it.

Are we taking away the ability to regulate stress from our kids by not allowing them to play enough? Looking at the number of anxiety disorders and depression in our society, one wonders if something is amiss. Seeing as one of the biggest reported fears of someone with an anxiety disorder is "the fear of losing control of their emotions", we can't help but ask: if we stand back and let our children play more, will they be more resilient and happier adults? We think the answer is yes.

Play and coping skills

In a pilot study conducted on preschool children in a child development center in Massachusetts, researchers wanted to measure whether there was a positive correlation between the level of playfulness in preschoolers and their coping skills. Using a Test of Playfulness (ToP) and Coping Inventory, the researchers cross-checked the children's playfulness and the quality of their coping skills. What they found was that there was a direct positive correlation between children's playfulness level and their ability to cope. The more they played and the better they were at playing, the better they were at coping. This led the researchers to believe that play had a direct effect on all of their life adaptability skills.

Another study conducted by Louise Hess, a professor of occupational therapy, and colleagues at a health institute in Palo Alto wanted to investigate the relationship between playfulness and coping skills in adolescent boys. They studied both normally developing ones and those with emotional problems. The researchers measured this with the ToP and Coping Inventory and their findings were almost identical to the preschool study. For both groups of boys, there was a direct and significant correlation between the level of playfulness and their ability to cope. They concluded that the use of play could be employed to improve coping skills and particularly to improve adaptability and being able to approach problems and goals in a more flexible way. This is fascinating if you think about it.

But it makes sense. Just look outside to see children swinging from bars or climbing trees or jumping from high places. They are testing dangerous situations and no one but the child himself knows the right dose or how to manage it. But it's important that they feel in control over the dose of stress they can handle. This in itself makes them feel more in control of their lives. Juvenile animals and primates do the same thing. They deliberately put themselves into dangerous situations, leaping and swinging from trees while twisting and turning, making it difficult to land. They are learning about fear and how to cope with it. It's the same with play fighting as mentioned earlier. The animals are putting themselves into both the subordinate and the attacker position to understand the emotional challenges of both.

For children, social situations are also stressful. Social play can bring on both conflict and cooperation. Fear and anger are just some of the emotions that a child must learn to cope with in order to keep playing. In play there is no such thing as getting excessive praise from the other kids like from their parents or their teachers. There are no special rules or special people in play. If someone feels too bullied or put down, they will quit. So rules have to be negotiated and renegotiated and players have to be aware of the emotional state of the other players in order to avoid someone getting upset and quitting, because if too many people quit, the game is over. Since children fundamentally want to play with each other, these situations make them practice getting along with others as equals. It makes them practice democracy. And democracy is an important value for the Danes.

Play Patrol and self-control

In many Danish schools, for example, there is a program in place called Play Patrol. Play Patrol is promoted by "Dansk Skoleidræt", which is a national sports organization whose main goal is to promote learning through sports, play and exercise for all students in the school.

The way it works is the school signs up for the program, then the selected students from the middle classes take part in a one-day training course. They are taught how to involve children of all ages in play and they learn a myriad of wonderful games and receive clothing and gear to help them stand out in the schoolyard. They also get a games folder and play bag that contains inspiration and tools to help them. They are taught how to include kids who are shyer and may have difficulty playing with others. Play Patrol creates more life on the playground both physically and socially. It ensures a better social environment in the schoolyard and it also helps prevent bullying. There is also something called "GameBoosters", which is exactly the same concept as Play Patrol but created for older students. No age is exempt from the importance of play!

"Both of my girls have Play Patrol in their school," Iben says, "and they love it. Ida, my older daughter, signed up to be a facilitator and it was a great learning experience for her because she got the chance to teach the younger pupils a lot of games. She really grew from the experience."

Playing between different ages like in Play Patrol and GameBoosters is a wonderful way to promote kids getting to the next zone of proximal development naturally. They have the ability to push and test themselves with the older kids in a way they wouldn't with their parents or teachers. They can practice different roles like mother, firefighter or family pet. Practicing more difficult roles and tasks between kids of different ages in play is a natural learning curve and also helps socialization.

Lev Vygotsky, the psychologist mentioned earlier, says that a lot of the value in children's play is based on the practice of self-control. He says that children's strong desire to keep the game going leads them to accept restrictions on their behavior that they would not accept in real life. This is how they acquire the capacities for self-control that are so crucial to social existence. They learn through play that self-control is a source of pleasure. Having self-control as an adult is a big factor in happiness and is partly developed through free play as a child. Learning to exercise self-control in order to keep a game going is much more meaningful than having control rules imposed upon us. Some say rules are made to be broken, but when a rule is discovered from within it becomes a core value rather than a boundary to push.

The truth behind Lego and playgrounds

Almost everyone has heard of Lego and played with the famous colorful building blocks at least once in their life. Ostensibly one of the most popular toys in history, Lego was dubbed "the toy of the century" at the start of the millennium by *Fortune* magazine. Originally made in wood and then plastic, Lego has never lost its fundamental building-block concept. Like the zone of proximal development, Lego can work for all ages. When the child is ready to take the next step towards a more challenging construction, to get to the next zone of proximal development, there are Legos made for taking that next step. It's a wonderful way to play with your child to gently help them master a new level. They can play on their own or with friends and countless hours have been spent playing with Lego all over the world.

The interesting fact most people don't know about Lego is that it comes from Denmark. Created by a Danish carpenter in his workshop in 1932, it was called Lego as a contraction of the words "Leg godt", which means to "play well". Even then, the idea of using your imagination to play freely was in full bloom.

Another of the world's biggest suppliers of play facilitators is a company called Kompan. Kompan creates outdoor playgrounds that have won numerous design awards for their simplicity, quality and functionality in supporting children's play. Their mission statement has been to promote healthy play as being important for children's learning. Their first playground was developed accidentally over 40 years ago when a young Danish artist noticed that his colorful art installation, created to brighten up a drab housing estate, was used more by children to play on than for the admiration of adults.

Kompan is now the number one playground supplier in the world. It's pretty fantastic to think that a country of only 5 million people is the world leader in both indoor and outdoor play supplies, and quite telling.

So the next time
When you see your children swinging from the branches, jumping off some rocks or play fighting with their friends and you want to intervene to save them, remember that this is their way of learning how much stress they can endure. When they are playing in a group with some difficult children and you want to protect them, remember that they are learning self-control and negotiation skills with all kinds of different personalities to keep the game alive. This is their way of testing their own abilities and developing adaptability skills in the process. The more they play, the more resilient and socially adept they will become in the long run. It's a very natural process. That's why the Danes have been so focused on play for all these years. They know it is a key element in long-term success and well-being in their children. Being able to "Leg godt" or "play well" is the building block to creating an empire of future happiness.

TIPS FOR PLAY

Now that we know play is healthy, how can we learn from the Danish way?

1. TURN IT OFF

Turn off the TV and the electronics! Imagination is the key for play to have its positive effects.

2. CREATE AN ENRICHING ENVIRONMENT

Studies show that a sensory-rich environment coupled with play facilitates cortical growth in the brain. Having a variety of materials around that can stimulate all of the senses—visual, auditory, tactile, etc.—enhances brain development during play.

3. USE ART

Children's brains grow when they make art. Therefore, don't show them how to do it, just put out the art supplies and let them create spontaneously.

4. Let them explore outside

Get them outside as much as possible to play in nature—in the woods, the park, the beach, wherever. Try to find safe areas where you aren't afraid to let them be free and explore the environment. These are places they can really use their imagination and have fun.

5. Mix children with different ages

Try to mix your children with other children of different ages. This enhances the zone of proximal development where one facilitates the other's learning, helping them get to a new level naturally. In this way, children learn to both star in the game as well as cooperate with the older ones. They learn to participate as well as challenge the game. This is teaching the self-control and negotiation skills so necessary in life.

6. Let them be free and forget the guilt

They don't need an adult-led activity or specific toys. The more you can let them be in control of their own play, using their imagination and doing it themselves, the better they will get at it. The skills they are learning are invaluable. We are so caught up in worrying about how many organized activities our children are involved in or what they are learning that we are forgetting the importance of letting them play freely. Stop feeling guilty that you aren't parenting by letting them play. Free play is what they are missing!

7. BE REAL

If you want to play with your kids, you must be 100 percent real in what you do. Don't be afraid to look silly. Let them guide. Stop worrying about what others think of you or what you think of yourself. Get down on their level and try to let go for even 20 minutes a day if it is difficult for you. Even a little playtime on their level is worth more than any toy you could buy.

8. LET THEM PLAY ALONE TOO

Playing alone is extremely important for kids. When they play with their toys, it is often their way of processing new experiences, conflicts and everyday events in their life. By engaging in fantasy play and using different voices, they can reenact what is happening in their world, which is hugely therapeutic. It is also great for developing their fantasy and imagination.

9. CREATE AN OBSTACLE COURSE

Try building obstacle courses with small stools and mattresses, or by any other means create space in the home so that children can move about and use their imagination. Let them be free to play and climb and explore and create without stressing over it.

10. Get other parents involved

Get other parents involved in the healthy play movement. The more parents who practice it, the more kids can be free to play together in non-adult-led activities. Pediatricians in the US have developed guidelines to persuade parents that play is healthy. Play is valuable for children and should be encouraged and discussed with others.

11. Avoid interacting too quickly

Try not to judge the other kids too harshly and intervene too quickly because you want to protect your kids from others. Sometimes it is learning how to deal with the more difficult children that provides them the biggest lessons in self-control and resilience.

12. Let go

Let your kids do things by themselves. When you feel the need to "save them", step back and take a breath. Remember that they are learning some of the most important skills to take them through life.

AUTHENTICITY
"No legacy is so rich as honesty."

SHAKESPEARE

Have you ever had that feeling when leaving a feel-good movie with a happy ending where you didn't actually feel that good? Where, despite the great ending, somewhere deep inside yourself you had the inkling that your life wasn't that great? Your job wasn't that great. Your relationship, your house, your car or your clothes just weren't as good as in the film? The whole thing actually didn't feel that realistic? But, you push it aside because, after all, it was a feel-good film, so no need to think too much about it. A large majority of Hollywood films are intended to make you feel good. But if art imitates life, one wonders how realistic these syrupy-sweet endings actually are.

Danish films, on the other hand, very often have dreary, sad or tragic endings. Much more rarely, one is left with the happy endings we are accustomed to. Many times, I have watched Danish films and waited to hear that soothing background music that would signal my suffering was about to end and everything would turn out all right after all. The boy would get the girl, the hero would save the day and all would be ok in the end. As an American, I almost felt it was my right to get a happy ending. But time and time again, the Danish films would touch on sensitive, real and painful issues that didn't wrap it up with a nice bow, lid closed, packaged up into the gift of a great life ahead. On the contrary, they left me standing with my raw emotions flapping in the wind, wondering what to do with them. How could Danes be so happy watching films like this? If art imitated life, what was I to think?

Silvia Knobloch-Westerwick, a professor of communications at Ohio State University, along with other researchers, has done research that has demonstrated that, contrary to popular belief, watching tragic or sad movies actually makes people happier by bringing attention to some of the more positive aspects of their own lives. It tends to make people reflect on their own relationships in a "count your blessings kind of way".

Eudaimonia and fairy-tale endings

Mary Beth Oliver, a professor of the positive psychology movement, has also identified many eudaimonic rewards of watching depressing, stressful or even horrific stories. Eudaimonia is a term coined by Aristotle. It is used to define the meaningfulness, insight and emotions that put us in touch with our own humanity. Eudaimonia can enrich us, leaving us fulfilled, touched and perhaps even teach us something about ourselves. Aristotle believed that happiness was more related to the virtue of our character and striving for human good. This involves being in touch with our authentic selves and reality, not numbing ourselves to it.

Looking to the fairy-tale world upon which our children are raised, Hans Christian Andersen is perhaps one of the most famous Danish writers in history. He is the author and forefather of numerous fairy tales like The Little Mermaid, The Ugly Duckling and The Emperor's New Clothes, just to name a few. These are tales that have been told the world over. But what most people don't realize is that a lot of Hans Christian Andersen's original fairy tales don't have our idea of a fairy-tale ending at all. They are tragedies. The Little Mermaid, for example, doesn't get the prince but rather turns into sea foam from sadness. Many of his fairy tales have merely been tailored to fit our cultural ideal of how we think things should be.

In the English translations of Andersen's fairy tales, adults have paid close attention to what they think children should be spared. In Denmark and in older versions, it is more up to the readers to come up with their own conclusions and judgments. Danes believe that tragedies and upsetting events are things we should talk about too. We learn more about character from our sufferings than our successes and therefore it's important to examine all parts of life. This is more authentic and it creates empathy and a deeper respect for humanity. It also helps us feel gratitude for the simple things in our life we sometimes take for granted by focusing too much on the fairy-tale life.

"I remember the story of the Little Match Girl as a child," Iben recounts. "It was so incredibly sad. The little girl ends up dying from hypothermia and I was filled with such sadness but oh, how I loved it!"

For Danes, well-being is very much tied to being an authentic, trusting and trustworthy person.

A few years ago, a study was conducted to examine the characters of different countries when no one was watching. Researchers lost more than 1,100 wallets in different countries to see how many would be returned. Each wallet contained 50 euro and the name and contact details of the owner of the wallet. The wallets were left on sidewalks and in phone booths, in front of office buildings, discount stores, churches, parking lots and restaurants. All in all, 56 percent of the wallets were returned but the results varied wildly from country to country. In the US, 67 percent of people returned the wallet. In Italy, only 35 percent of people returned the wallet, but in Denmark, the return rate was an impressive 100 percent!

Why people returned the wallets was revealed in the interviews afterwards. For almost all of the people who returned the wallets, young and old, their motivation was due to their parents instilling in them the desire to do the right thing. For many others, empathy was a fundamental reason. They genuinely cared that the owner might need that money.

We are so busy teaching kids how to be smart and to be good and even be the best at things (because being the best will bring happiness, right?) that many of us have forgotten the importance of teaching good, solid, honest character values.

Society has a lot of invisible norms and expectations, pushing us to live in often oppressive and restrictive ways. We believe we must live up to an idea of ourselves when what we really need to do is to learn to listen to our hearts and trust our feelings. If we teach our children to feel inwardly and act on it, the challenges and downs of life won't topple them. They will know that they have acted in accordance with what feels right through time. They will know how to recognize their own limits and respect them. It is the inner compass we must instill with strong values. An authentic self-esteem based on values becomes the most powerful guiding force in one's life, much more resistant to external pressures.

Parenting with authenticity
Parenting with authenticity is the first step to guiding a child to be courageously true to themselves and others. Being a model of emo-

tional health is powerful parenting. Not perfection but emotional honesty. It is what children need so desperately. Children are always observing how you feel anger, joy, frustration, contentment and success and how you express it in the world. We have to model honesty for our children and let them know that it is ok to feel all of their emotions. Many parents find it easier to manage their children's happy feelings, but when it comes to the difficult ones, such as anger, aggressivity and anxiety, it becomes more difficult. Therefore, children learn less about these emotions, which may affect their ability to regulate them in the future. Conceptualizing all emotions early on makes it easier to maneuver in the world.

When going through a difficult time, for example, smiling and saying everything is ok is not always the best course of action. Self-deception is the worst kind of deception and it is a dangerous message to teach our kids. They will learn to do the same. Self-deception is confusing because it makes us ignore our real feelings and can cause us to make choices based on external influences rather than on our own authentic desires. This leads us down paths to places we don't actually want to be in life. And that is how we end up unhappy. It's that moment when many people look at their lives and say "Hold on, is this what I really wanted? Or is this what I thought I was supposed to want?"

Parenting with authenticity is the first step to guiding a child to be courageously true to themselves and others.

Authenticity is searching your heart and gut for what is right for you and your family and not being afraid to follow through with it. It's allowing yourself to be in touch with your own emotions and not bury or numb them but act on them. These things take courage and strength but the payoff is huge. Learning to act on intrinsic goals, like improving relationships or engaging in hobbies you love, rather than extrinsic goals, like buying a new car, is what is proven to create true well-being.

Thus, having the bigger house or more stuff or enrolling your kids in all the right activities can be a self-deceptive pitfall. Pushing your own or others' dreams onto yourself and your kids, rather than listening carefully to their desires and respecting their zones of proximal development, is another pitfall. Being too pressured or praised, children may learn to do things for external recognition rather than internal satisfaction, which becomes a default setting for life. It encourages extrinsic goals: needing something outside of themselves to make them happy. This may bring success by some people's standards, but it won't necessarily bring them that deep sense of internal happiness and well-being we are all striving for. As we saw earlier, it can actually breed anxiety and depression.

The Danish way of authentic praise

Being humble is a very important value in Denmark. This dates far back into history and is a part of their cultural heritage. This value of humility is about knowing who you are so well that you don't need others to make you feel important. Therefore, they try not to overload their children with compliments.

"I tell my daughters they can do anything with hard work," Iben says. "They know they have to develop themselves and grow and I encourage that. But I try not to overuse praise with them. I think that if kids can't make sense of too many compliments, they can sound empty and hollow."

For example, if a child scribbles a drawing very quickly and gives it to a Danish parent, they probably wouldn't say "Wow! Great job! You are such a good artist!" They are more likely to ask about the drawing itself. "What is it?" "What were you thinking about when you drew this?" "Why did you use those colors?" Or perhaps they would just say "thank you" if it was a gift.

Focusing on the task rather than over-complimenting the child is a much more Danish approach.

This helps to focus on the work involved but it also inadvertently teaches humility. Helping children build on the feeling of being able to master a skill rather than already being a master provides a more solid foundation to stand on and grow from. This promotes inner strength and resilience.

And, in fact, new and very interesting research supports this idea. The way we praise our children does have a profound effect on resilience!

Fixed mindset versus a growth mindset

In America, we believe that praising kids for how smart they are builds their confidence and motivation to learn. We are rather obsessed with the idea of talent and genius and innate abilities. We freely praise our children and others because we think it is helpful. But three decades of research done by Stanford psychologist Carol S. Dweck has proven otherwise.

Praise is very connected to how kids view their intelligence. If kids are constantly praised for being naturally smart, talented or gifted (sound familiar?), they develop what is called a fixed mindset (their intelligence is fixed and they have it).

Children, however, who are told that their intelligence can be developed with work and education develop what is called a growth mindset (they can develop their skills because they are working very hard).

What findings show is that kids who have a fixed mindset, who have constantly been told they are smart, tend to care first and foremost about how they will be judged: smart or not smart. They are afraid to have to exert too much effort because effort makes them feel dumb. They believe that if you have the ability, you shouldn't need the effort. And since they have always been told they have the ability, they are afraid that by needing to really try hard to do something they will lose their smart status.

Kids with a growth mindset, alternatively, care about learning. Those who have been encouraged to focus on their efforts rather than their intelligence see effort as a positive thing. It sparks their intelligence and causes it to grow. These students increase their efforts in the face of failure and look for new learning strategies rather than giving up. This is the epitome of resilience.

The real catalyst for outstanding achievement
Growing research in psychology and neuroscience also supports the idea that a growth mindset is the real catalyst for outstanding achievement. Studies of the brain show that our mind has much more plasticity over time than we ever dreamed. The basic facets of

our intelligence can be improved through learning even into old age. It's the persistence and dedication when faced with obstacles that are the key ingredients to overall success in a lot of areas.

This is really eye-opening. How many smart and talented people do you know who have never lived up to their potential because they had a fixed mindset about being naturally smart?

Some interesting studies conducted on 5th graders by mindset expert Dweck and colleagues aimed to show how praise affects students' performance. Groups of students were given specific kinds of tasks to work on and then received different kinds of praise for their work. Some students heard things like "You must be smart at solving these problems" (encouraging a fixed mindset) and others heard "You must have worked hard on solving these problems" (encouraging a growth mindset). Afterwards, the students were asked to agree or disagree with certain statements, like "Your intelligence is something basic about you that you can't really change." The students who were praised for being smart agreed with these statements much more than the ones who were praised for their effort.

In a follow-up study, the students were asked to give their definition of intelligence. The students who had been praised for intelligence said they thought intelligence was an innate trait that was fixed, whereas the ones who were praised for effort thought it was something you could develop with work.

Students were then given the option to work on an easy problem or a difficult one. The students who were praised for intelligence chose to do the easy problem rather than the hard one to ensure a perfect performance. The ones praised for effort chose the challenging one with the opportunity to learn. Afterwards, all the students were given a complicated task to work on. The children with the fixed mindset lost their confidence and enjoyment the minute they had difficulties solving the problem. For them, success meant being innately smart so struggling meant they were not. The growth mindsets, alternatively, didn't lose their confidence and were eager to try to solve the problems.

When the problems were made easier again, the students praised for their intelligence had already lost their confidence and motivation from the harder problems and did badly overall. As a group, they did worse on the same kind of problems they had been given in the beginning, while the group praised for efforts continually improved and did an excellent job overall.

Perhaps what was most interesting, though, was when asked anonymously to report their scores, the fixed mindsets lied about their results more than 40 percent of the time. Their self-image was so tied up in their scores that they were afraid to admit failure, whereas the growth mindsets lied 10 percent of the time. Studies conducted on cheating in schools confirm that students today are far more likely to cheat in order to get high grades than in previous generations.

We think telling kids how smart they are boosts confidence but in the face of difficulties, it actually makes them lose their confidence! Praising students for their intelligence doesn't give them the motivation or resilience crucial to being successful, but rather can give them a fixed mindset full of vulnerability. In contrast, effort or "process" praise—praise for engagement, perseverance, strategies, improvement and so on—fosters motivation and resilience. It tells kids what they've done to be successful and what they need to do to be successful in the future.

Interestingly enough, a recent *New York Times* article reports that even businesses nowadays are looking for people with a growth mindset rather than a fixed mindset. Since people with a growth mindset are much better at fostering teamwork and resolving challenges without getting stressed, they are much more interesting for an organization. The innately talented, or the fixed mindsets, are more egocentric and concerned about being the biggest star in the organization. It's the ones who can tackle a task with perseverance and resilience, incorporating others with gratitude, that will ultimately make it to CEO status.

Some examples of process praise are:

—"I like the way you tried putting the puzzle pieces together again and again. You didn't give up and you found a way to put it together!"

—"You practiced that dance so many times and the effort really showed today! You danced really well!"

—"I am so proud of you for how you shared your snack with your brother. It makes me so happy to see you sharing."

—"It was a long, difficult assignment but you stayed at it and got it done. I am so proud of you for how you stayed focused and kept working. Well done!"

TIPS FOR AUTHENTICITY

How do we use the Danish Way to teach authenticity?

1. No SELF-DECEPTION

Be honest with yourself first and foremost. Learn how to look at your own life authentically. Being able to detect and define your own emotions and how you truly feel is a huge milestone. Teaching emotional honesty to your kids and preventing them from becoming self-deceptive is a great gift. Listening to and expressing one's own true thoughts and feelings is what keeps us on the right track to going for what makes us happy in life. Being honest with ourselves is how we calibrate our internal compasses to go in the right direction. Our internal compass is what guides us through life. If we calibrate it wrongly or dishonestly or refuse to listen to it, we risk getting lost.

2. BE AUTHENTIC

If your kids ask a question, give them an honest answer. Of course, you have to be age appropriate and up to their level of understanding. Being sincere in your responses is true for all aspects of life, even the difficult ones. By not being authentic, you undermine your child's ability to sense what is true and false. They are incredible lie detectors and they can feel unstable if you are being fake.

3. Use examples from your own life to be authentic

Use examples from your own life of what you experienced as a child whenever you feel it could be useful. Whether it be at the doctor's office or during a difficult situation or just having fun, kids like to hear about your experiences and how you felt when you were little, particularly when it is true and heartfelt. This gives them a better understanding of who you are and it lets them know that their situation is normal even if they are scared or happy or sad.

4. Teach honesty

Talk with your child about how important honesty is in your family. Make it a value. Let them know you put more emphasis on honesty than on the punishment for dishonest behavior. If you confront your kids accusingly with anger or threats and are punitive when they lie, then they are afraid to tell the truth. If you make it safe for them, they will be honest. Remember, it takes a lot to confess or tell the truth for anyone at any age. It doesn't always come naturally. It's up to us to teach them to be courageous enough be honest and vulnerable and confess when necessary. Be non-judgmental. This kind of honest relationship, if fostered well, will be paramount during the teenage years.

5. READ STORIES THAT ENCOMPASS ALL EMOTIONS

Read all kinds of stories to your child. Don't be afraid of them if they don't all have happy endings. Actively choose stories that have difficult topics too and stories that don't conclude for you in a perfect way. Children learn a lot from sadness and tragedy (being age appropriate, of course) and it opens up honest communication between you about different aspects of life that are just as important as the Prince getting the Princess. Being exposed to peaks and valleys of life encourages empathy, resilience and eudaimonia (feelings of meaningfulness and happiness for our own lives).

6. USING PROCESS PRAISE: HOW TO BUILD A GROWTH MINDSET RATHER THAN A FIXED MINDSET

Remember that the praise is quality, not quantity. Keep the praise focused on the process or effort children put in rather than on innate abilities.

"You studied hard for your test, and your improvement shows it. You went over the material many times, made cue cards and quizzed yourself. That really worked!"

Try to think up some more examples of process praise. Practice makes perfect. The more you try to use process praise, the better you will get at it. See if you can avoid saying "you are so smart" too much. By focusing on the effort involved, you will give your children the tools to believe that it is the perseverance, not the innate ability, that matters. In the long run, they will have a stronger self-esteem because of it.

7. Don't overuse praise

Don't overuse praise for things that are too easy. This can teach your child that he is only praiseworthy when he completes a task quickly, easily and perfectly and that does not help him embrace challenges. If, for example, a child gets an A too easily without much effort, try saying, "Well that was way too easy for you! Why don't we try doing something more challenging that you can learn from?" The goal is not to make easily performed tasks the basis for our admiration.

8. Focus on effort

Be careful praising for failures or mistakes. Saying things like "Well done!" "You did your best!" "Better luck next time!" can be heard as pity. Focus on what they did accomplish and how it can be worked on—"I know you missed the goal but it was very close! Let's get out and practice next week and you'll get it next time! Remember, practice is the key!" By focusing on the effort involved in learning, we create a growth mindset. This mindset is helpful in all aspects of life from work to relationships.

9. TEACH CHILDREN NOT TO COMPARE THEMSELVES WITH OTHERS

They need to realize themselves whether they did their best on a project or if they feel they can do more. Are they satisfied with the job? It is that feeling that they have to learn to rely on and gauge themselves by, not on how they compare to others. Not everyone can be the best at everything but you can be the best for yourself and this fosters well-being.

10. EMPHASIZE YOUR UNDERSTANDING BY SAYING "FOR ME"

Try to remember to say "for me" after a sentence to emphasize your understanding that your reality isn't necessarily your child's reality. For example, if you have an argument with your child about food being too hot, it is important to remember that although it isn't too hot for you, it may be too hot for your child. Saying "The food isn't too hot for me" lets them know that you understand this. Or instead of saying "The weather isn't cold," you could say "The weather isn't cold for me." "For me" after the sentence allows your child to know that you understand that they may have a different experience of the world than you do and you respect this. This builds trust and respect.

Reframing

"It's snowing still," said Eeyore gloomily.
"So it is."
"And freezing."
"Is it?"
"Yes," said Eeyore. "However," he said,
brightening up a little, "we haven't had an
earthquake lately."

A. A. MILNE. WINNIE THE POOH

I remember the first time it occurred to me that my husband was doing something differently with our children than I did. Whenever there was a negative situation of some kind, I tended to respond a little too quickly. With exasperation, I would throw up my hands. "She won't do it! She never listens!" He, on the other hand, always had more patience, more calm and a magical sentence on hand that could amaze even me. It was like a window opening up into a darkened room shedding new light onto a discussion I had previously seen no possibility in. He could put something unpleasant in a more positive light. He could make a black-and-white situation seem a little grayer. Pain became less painful and anger more tempered. I noticed his family and friends doing the same with their children. Where was this magical phrasebook the Danes were using?

One morning listening to him delicately alter my daughter's language around her fear of spiders, it hit me how powerful this influence was going to be for her future. As I watched her carefully study the spider with him and marvel at it, instead of screaming in fear saying "Eew!" it struck me that the "Danish Way" of language use was huge. Because it wasn't just about the language, it was about using the language to create a perception shift.

You see, the way we see life and filter our day-to-day experiences affects the way we feel in general. Many of us are unaware that the way we see things is an unconscious choice. We feel that our perception of life is the truth. It's our truth. We don't think of our perception as a learned way of seeing things (often picked up from our parents and our culture). We see it as just the way things are. And this set way of "the way things are" is called a frame. And this frame through which we see the world is our perception. And what we perceive as the truth feels like the truth.

But what if we could see the truth in a new way? What if we could take the truth as we see it and put it into a new mental frame? A broader, more open-minded frame and hang it back on the wall? If we look at that picture we call "the truth" again, how would we see it?

Try to imagine we are standing in an art gallery. The picture is hanging on the wall and there is a guide who is pointing out the subtle details of the picture to us. We begin to notice things we hadn't seen before. These new details we see were clearly there before but we missed them because we were too focused on what we thought was the most obvious theme. It was a negative picture, we concluded, and that's what it was. The man was mean, the woman was helpless and the mood was somber. You are about to move on but now you realize, with the help of the guide, that there is an entirely different storyline to focus on in the picture. You see there are jovial people arriving in the window behind the couple bearing gifts. The man is being bitten by a dog, which is why he looks mean, and the woman is being helpful, not helpless. There is a child laughing in the background you hadn't noticed and the light streaming through the window is extraordinary. In the very same picture, there are many other things to focus on you hadn't even seen. It feels exhilarating to experience this mental shift and discovery. Our memory of that picture will now be completely different and the way we share our observations about it with others will be too. With practice, finding these alternative storylines becomes a skill, not a struggle. And the guide pointing out these alternate storylines in the future will be you.

Realistic optimism
Do you think that the ability to reframe a stressful situation—a family issue, a co-worker problem, a disobedient child—like we did with this picture could actually change our well-being? The answer is yes, yes and a resounding yes! And it's something the Danes have been doing for centuries. They teach their children this invaluable skill and learning how to reframe early makes them grow up to be naturally better at it as adults. And being a master reframer is a cornerstone of resilience.

Ask a Dane how they think the weather is when it is freezing, gray and raining out and they will unwittingly answer:

"Well, it's a good thing I am at work!"
"Glad I am not on holiday!"
"I am looking forward to cozying at home inside tonight with the family."
"There isn't bad weather, only bad clothing!"

Try to get a Dane to focus on something really negative in any kind of topic and you will be mystified at how they are able to find a more positive outlook on the conversation.

"Too bad it's the last weekend of vacation."
"Yes, but it's the first weekend of the rest of our lives!"

And we don't mean to say that the Danes have an exaggerated over-the-top positive outlook with reframing. The Danes aren't floating around on a buoyant cloud of optimism often associated with super happy people. The "Oh my god, everything is so great and wonderful!" types. The ones who look like their smile is glued on and they are high on life all the time. No, Danes don't pretend that negativity doesn't exist. They just point out in a rather matter-of-fact way that another side also exists that you may never have even considered thinking about. They choose to focus on the good in people instead of the bad. They change their expectations to focus on the bigger picture rather than getting trapped by one aspect of an argument and they generally tend to be more tempered in their assumptions. Danes are what psychologists call "realistic optimists".

Realistic optimists are different than those overly optimistic people with the glued-on smiles. Those people who sometimes appear to be fake because life sounds too perfect. The problem with being overly positive and optimistic is the same problem at the opposite end of the spectrum as people who are overly negative and pessimistic. Very negative people tend to ignore positive information, which can bring them down and prevent them from seeing a positive reality. Overly positive people, on the other hand, tend to ignore negative information, which can make them oblivious to important negative realities. It's risky to force yourself to believe "Everything is great!" and saying "No, there's no problem at all" when really there is. Underestimating negative situations has the potential to deliver a much bigger blow when hit with one. This is related to the self-deception we talked about earlier in Authenticity. Being in touch with reality but focusing on the more positive angles is much more in line with being a realistic optimist.

Realistic optimists merely filter out unnecessary negative information. They learn to tune out negative words and occurrences and develop a habit of interpreting ambiguous situations in a more positive manner. They don't see things as only bad or good or black or white but rather realize that there are many shades in between. Focusing on the less negative aspects of situations and finding a grayer middle ground reduces anxiety and increases well-being.

The skill of reframing

Numerous organizations for adults in America are training their workers on the skill of reinterpreting information called reframing because it is seen as a key trait in resilience. In a *Harvard Business Review* article, Dean M. Becker, the founder of resilience firm Adaptive Learning Systems, is quoted as saying, "More than education, more than experience, more than training, a person's level of resilience will determine who succeeds and who fails. That's true in the cancer ward, it's true in the Olympics, and it's true in the boardroom." Being able to reframe negative situations is a key element to being resilient.

Numerous studies show that when we deliberately reinterpret an event to feel better about it, it decreases activity in areas of the brain involved in the processing of negative emotions such as the amygdala and the insula and increases activity in areas of the brain involved in cognitive control and adaptive integrations.

In one reframing study, two groups of participants were shown pictures of angry faces. The first group was told to think that the people in the pictures just had a bad day and their faces had nothing to do with them. The other group was told to feel whatever emotions the faces elicited. What they found was that the group that had been trained to adjust their attitude about the angry faces weren't disturbed at all and, in fact, recorded electrical brain activity showed that the reframing had wiped out the negative signals in their brain, whereas the other group that felt whatever came to mind were disturbed by the faces. We feel what we think.

In another study done by Stanford University, researchers exposed different groups of participants with phobias to spiders and snakes. One group was trained to reframe their experience and the other

Do you think that the ability to reframe a stressful situation—a family issue, a co-worker problem, a disobedient child—like we did with this picture could actually change our well-being? The answer is yes, yes and a resounding yes!

wasn't. The trained group showed significantly less fear and panic than the control group and the results caused lasting changes in emotional responding when they were exposed again later to the spiders and snakes. This demonstrates the durable effects of cognitive reframing.

So not only does reframing change our brain chemistry but it helps how we interpret pain, fear, anxiety and the like. And this reframing is directly related to the language we use both out loud and in our head.

The limitations of limiting language

Limiting language, on the other hand, has the opposite effect. Saying things like "I hate flying," or "I am terrible at cooking," or "I have no willpower, that's why I am so fat," is limiting language. "I really enjoy traveling once I get off the plane," "I prefer using recipes when I cook," "I am trying to eat healthy and walk more now," are completely different ways of looking at the same things. It's less black and white, less limiting and has a completely different feel. Our language is a choice, you see, and it's crucial because it forms the frame through which we see the world. By reframing what we say into something more supportive and less defining, we actually change the way we feel.

Some researchers think that reframing is so beneficial to humans that it should be in the water we drink. Just like we add fluoride to water or vitamin D to cornflakes to improve human health, they believe that if reframing were done with the same frequency that we drink water, it would have a huge impact on the emotional well-being of our society. Looking to the Danes, you can't help but think they have a good point.

Where the actual ability to reframe comes from in Denmark is unclear. Realistic optimism just seems to be a default setting in their society. These language choices associated with reframing are passed on through generations. Most Danes are unaware that they have this gift—it is so much a part of the way they are. And we are convinced it is one of the reasons Danes are constantly voted so happy.

How reframing works with children

Reframing with children is about the adult helping the child to shift focus from what they think they can't do to what they can do. The adult helps the child see situations from different angles and gets them to focus on the less negative outcomes or conclusions. With practice, this can become a default setting.

When you or your children use limiting language like "I hate this," "I can't do it," "I am not good at that," etc., you create negative identity conclusions. Negative identity conclusions occur when events happen together in sequences according to a plot or theme. The plot may have us convinced that we aren't good at anything or we are doing everything wrong. The more a child is told limiting beliefs about "how they are" or "how they should do or feel things" in all kinds of situations, they begin to build coping strategies based on a distrust of their own abilities in the face of new challenges. "She isn't very good at sports," "He is so messy," "She is too sensitive." These are all very defining. The more of these children get, the more negative conclusions about themselves they get. And this is because we, as human beings, always try to find meaning in action. If we don't understand something, we create our own conclusions, and these conclusions are often negative beliefs like "Since I don't get it, it must be me who is wrong."

To reduce the problem, it helps to find and create a different narrative for your children. Leading them to a new, broader or more ambiguous picture conclusion about themselves helps them to reframe. And this skill will transfer over into how they learn to see and interpret life and others as well.

In Iben's practice as a narrative therapist, she focuses a lot on reframing and, even more in-depth, on "reauthoring". She helps people look at the beliefs they have about themselves and the beliefs they put onto their kids without realizing it. Saying things like "He is antisocial," "She isn't very academic," "He is terrible at math," or "She is so selfish," are all statements that become behavior your children try to make sense of and identify with. Children can hear you say these things much more often than parents realize they can. Soon, they believe that it must be how they are. When new behavior doesn't fit into this label, they don't even try to make sense of it anymore because they have already identified themselves as being antisocial or terrible at math. The language we use is extremely powerful. It is the frame through which we perceive and describe ourselves and our picture of the world.

Allan Holmgren, a well-known Danish psychologist, believes that our reality is created in the language we use. All change involves a change in language. A problem is only a problem if it is referred to as a problem.

The power of labels
Many of these labels and storylines, you see, follow us into adulthood. So much of what we think about ourselves as adults comes from the labeling we were given as children—lazy, sensitive, selfish,

stupid, smart. Think about it: what are your beliefs about who you are and how much of them came from what you were told as a child? Many of us continue to live up to and compare ourselves with these labels unconsciously for the rest of our lives. By separating ourselves from these labels, we open up new paths of change for ourselves and our children.

This is a very interesting concept when you really think about it. Consider how common it is to hear people talking about kids as having a disorder these days, even if they have never even seen a psychologist. It seems like it has become completely natural to talk about children, our own and others, as having psychological problems. Shyness is described as Asperger's, kids who have lots of energy are considered ADHD, children who don't constantly smile must be showing symptoms of depression and the latest thing we heard was a quiet child who was described as having sensory overload disorder. Sensory overload disorder? This was news! The parents were worried, the daughter was worried and it was worrying to think how labeling her like that would affect her for the rest of her life.

Saying so nonchalantly that children have a psychological problem as if they are hungry or cold is very serious. Not only does it belittle the severity and seriousness of those who truly suffer from these disorders, but it also labels children unfairly. When they hear a plot line repeated about their lives, they begin to associate themselves with these labels and draw identity conclusions from them. These narratives become their life story and it is very hard to get out of them. So the very things we don't like in ourselves or in our children, we are encouraging by saying them and repeating them. By reframing, or reauthoring, we can help rewrite our own and our children's future.

Reauthoring

Iben gives an example of how she helps adults and children with reauthoring in her practice. "When someone comes to me who is unhappy with the way their life is going, I try to talk about the things they say about themselves. We talk about their negative identity conclusions and try to separate them from these labels. One of my patients, for example, said that she was lazy and scatterbrained and it was ruining her life. So I asked her about this and what kinds of feelings this label evoked. She said it made her feel awful, especially when she would forget something or get lost or sleep in late. These behaviors just enforced the bad feeling. Being lazy made her feel like a failure and that she had no willpower. Therefore, every time she said 'I am lazy and scatterbrained,' she was unconsciously reiterating this plot line in her head to others and making it more prevalent in her life.

At this point, I used externalization language. This is language that separates the person from the problem. Laziness is not something in the genes but rather something that can affect people at different times. By separating the person from the problem, it makes us more able to feel like an active agent in our own life to combat the problem.

I tried to make her visualize laziness and describe it. Is it a dark cloud? Is it stifling you? What kinds of feelings does it make you feel when it arises? She said it was like someone was holding her down. It was heavy air on top of her and she was paralyzed to turn off the alarm. It was foggy when she tried to read a map. It held her down when she wanted to exercise. It made her feel undependable, incapable and pathetic.

We then moved on to talking about the opposite feelings of laziness. We talked about what she valued in herself. We talked about what she would like her life to be if she could shake off this heavy air that fell upon her.

We then drew on past experiences to find a different story about her life. It turned out that she had phenomenal communication and creativity skills. She was funny and a deeply loyal friend. She was very skilled in cooking and music and she had plenty of experiences to pull from where she hadn't been lazy at all. We talked at length about those experiences. So instead of focusing on the negative identity conclusion of being lazy and scatterbrained, we focused on the values and skills we wanted to "thicken" in her narrative. The more we focused on talking about the values and skills she liked about herself, the more positive and loving the storyline about herself became. Slowly, she began to define herself in a new way.

She was now creative, strong and dependable, and she felt she had the tools to reframe her perspective of life and her identity conclusions even more. With practice, her outer voice turned into her inner voice. The problem was now the problem, it wasn't who she was anymore. I doubt she will ever define herself as lazy and scatterbrained again. The power of that defining language was so much bigger than she had ever realized."

Thus, reframing and reauthoring isn't about eliminating negative events in our life, rather, it is about placing less importance on them and focusing more on the aspects we do like. Just like in the painting from the beginning of the chapter: by being open to changing the frame, we can see a bigger picture and practice concentrating on other details that tell a different story. We can change our whole experience of life into something better. This is exactly the same for kids. We, as adults, are the guides to pointing out a more positive and loving storyline for them too.

How to limit limiting language

Saying things like "She is such a picky eater," "He hates reading," or "He never listens," is enforcing that behavior to be who children are. The reality is, every behavior has a feeling or a mood behind it. It isn't fixed. Maybe they are tired or hungry or upset about something? The more we can separate the behavior from the child, the more we can change how we see them and, thus, how they see themselves. This lets them know that they are ok and the behavior is not their destiny. Labels, as we have seen, can become a self-fulfilling prophecy.

A stubborn child may be very difficult at times, but try to see the bigger picture and what led to that behavior. Instead of saying how impossible the child is and making them a problem, try noting the other sides of the story. Maybe the child who refuses to eat had a snack before dinner and really isn't very hungry. Maybe the child who won't get dressed is in the boundary pushing age and doesn't understand why socks are important. And moreover, what are the other sides of that stubborn behavior? Perhaps the child is very persistent and decisive and shows great leadership skills? Persistence is a powerful characteristic that takes us far in life. Maybe the distracted child is very creative and really loves art?

By talking about and nurturing the positive aspects of an unpleasant behavior, we are helping our child focus on the better storyline too. This also prevents a lot of power struggles and leads to happier parents and children.

The Danish way of reframing

Danes, on the whole, use less limiting language and don't tell children how they are or what they think they should do or feel in different situations. You don't hear a lot of adult opinions being placed on children. "You shouldn't be like that." "Don't cry." "You should be happy!" "He is mean!" "He shouldn't be like that." "You should tell him next time!"

They tend to focus more on using supporting language, which leads children to understand the reasons for their emotions and actions. If they are upset or angry, for example, they try to help a child become aware of why they feel that way rather than saying how they should or shouldn't be feeling.

"What's wrong?"
"Nothing."
"You look like something is wrong—is there?"
"Yeah."
"What's going on?"
"I don't know."
"Are you sad? Angry? Happy?"
"I am sad."
"Why do you feel sad?"
"I am sad because Gary took my doll at playtime."
"He took your doll. Why do you think he took your doll?"
"Because he is mean."
"You think he is mean? Is Gary always mean?"
"Yes."
"But last week you said you played a lot with Gary, right?"
"Yes."
"Was he mean then?"

"No."

"Ok, so sometimes Gary is nice?"

"Yes. Sometimes he is nice."

They are good at helping their children conceptualize their emotions and then guiding them into finding something nicer or more constructive, instead of a disparaging or limited belief. This is the heart of reframing.

"So what happened when he took your doll?"

"I cried."

"So you were sad he took your doll. I can understand that. What do you think you could do differently next time if Gary takes your doll so you won't be sad?"

"I can tell him to give it back. Or I can tell the teacher."

"I think telling him to give it back sounds like a good solution. Does Gary like to play with dolls?"

"Sometimes."

"Is there anything else you could do other than ask for it back?"

"Maybe we could play together with the dolls."

"That sounds like a great solution. We know Gary is actually a sweet boy so next time you can ask if he wants to play dolls too."

"Yes!"

Finding the nicer side of things can be done with all kinds of situations, not only with people. With practice it becomes much easier to scan a scene and find the hidden details that reframe a situation into something more pleasant. It can even be fun to do.

Once a child finds a better alternative storyline, try to repeat it for them so it sticks. But the solution should ultimately come from them.

This builds real self-esteem because they become the master of their own emotional responses. They aren't told how to feel and act.

If we hold onto the good in people, to separate actions from the person, we teach our children that we forgive them when they themselves misbehave. Imagine if we had said that what Gary did was ridiculous and mean. Children will remember that. When it's our own child who is doing something similar next time, they know that we judge. If we trust other people and know how to forgive, we teach our children that we also forgive them when they misbehave. If we maintain that it is human to fail, and that we can see other positive things despite that, our children will also be gentler on themselves when they fail.

Another way of reframing is to use humor. If you find yourself on the side of a soccer field and your child played badly and says so— "I played terribly,"—a typical way of responding might be, "No, you didn't! You played great! The field was slippery! You'll win next time! You win some, you lose some!"

A Danish way of reframing with humor might be something like the following:

"I played terribly."
"Did you break your leg?"
"No, but I am a terrible player."
"But you didn't break your leg, did you? Are you sure?" (go down to check the leg) "Well, at least you didn't break your leg!"
"Ha ha, I am terrible at soccer. I should quit. I hate it."
"You hate it? Yes, you did play pretty badly today, but remember last week when you scored two goals?"

"Oh yeah but..."

"Remember how you felt when you scored those goals?"

"Pretty good."

"I think I remember you dancing around the field and singing. Did you hate soccer then?"

"No."

"Exactly, so just remember how you felt last week and let's think of what we can do to help you play better next time."

"Practice more I guess."

"Yes and let's go have pizza and celebrate the fact that you didn't break your leg!"

"Some days are bad, some are good."

Notice that in this example, the parent doesn't ignore the fact that the child played badly. The parent acknowledges it but uses humor to show how much worse the situation could be as well as lead the child to positive feelings he or she did have about playing soccer the week before. This is being a realistic optimist. By acknowledging reality, you can still eliminate the unnecessary negative words and focus on the good feelings rather than the bad through humor or focus on another time of feeling good. It's all in the way you frame it. And practice makes perfect!

"Reframing can be extremely powerful in building children's self-esteem because much of reframing involves changing how you see your child's behavior," Iben says. "You are not the problem, the problem is the problem." If you choose to look at the positive aspects of any child's behavior, you are giving them the tools to deal with their own uniqueness.

If we trust other people and know how to forgive, we teach our children that we also forgive them when they misbehave.

TIPS FOR REFRAMING

How can we practice the Danish Way of reframing?

1. PAY ATTENTION TO YOUR NEGATIVITY

Practice noticing when you have a negative thought pattern. Just try to notice it and see how often you are using negativity to view a situation. Try to come up with different ways of looking at things that upset you, like fears or worries, as an exercise. Try taking a step back in perspective and see if you can find understanding and another way to see things or a way to focus on a more positive aspect.

2. PRACTICE REFRAMING

Think about how realistic your thoughts are and try changing the phrasing. Consider the following sentences: "I never have time to exercise. I am so fat." "I am a terrible writer." "My mother-in-law is so annoying." Now try turning them into a different sentence. "I do manage to exercise at least once a week and I am trying to eat salads for lunch, which feels good." "I am a pretty decent writer once I get in the zone." "I love my mother-in-law even if we have our differences. She is a great grandmother to the kids." It can be challenging to do but we know it makes a difference in our brain chemistry and this affects our well-being! At first it can even feel silly to do it, but the better you get at reframing, the better you will feel. Everything we see and say negatively about ourselves, our family, our anxieties and fears passes directly onto our kids, so give the gift of reframing to yourself and your children and make them naturally better at coping with life.

3. USE LESS LIMITING LANGUAGE

Try to eliminate the black-and-white, limiting language. I hate this, I love that, I always, I never, I should, I shouldn't. I am like this, she is like that, etc., etc. Limiting language leaves little room to maneuver and is only viewing things from one's own angle. Try to use more tempered, less severe language. Use less judgment and more acceptance and you will find yourself in fewer power struggles with your kids and your partner.

4. TRY EXTERNALIZATION LANGUAGE: SEPARATE THE ACTIONS FROM THE PERSON

Instead of saying "She is lazy," or "He is aggressive," try seeing laziness and aggressivity as something that is external rather than innate. "She is affected by laziness," or "He is struck by moments of aggressivity," is very different from labeling as "how they are".

5. REWRITE YOUR CHILD'S NARRATIVE TO BE MORE LOVING

Make a list of your child's most negative qualities and behaviors and write them out as a sentence. "She isn't very academic." "I think he has ADHD." "She is so stubborn." Then try to rewrite the sentences identifying the source of those behaviors. Like the one who isn't very academic may love reading and be extremely social. The one who has ADHD may be energetic and a fantastic drummer. The stubborn one may be a patient hard worker who doesn't give up. Try focusing on the positive side to your children's behavior so they feel appreciated for their uniqueness rather than labeled negatively. Rewrite the negative identity conclusions for yourself and your children and separate the behavior from the child. Then we all have the ability to grow and rewrite more loving narratives about ourselves and our children.

6. USE SUPPORTING LANGUAGE

Help your child by using supporting language rather than limiting language. Ask questions to help them identify their emotions behind the actions. Help them identify their intentions and the intentions of others so they understand how to lead themselves out of situations.

7. USE HUMOR

Use humor to reframe but don't negate negativity.

EMPATHY

"The best and most beautiful things in the world cannot be seen or even touched. They must be felt with the heart."

HELEN KELLER

For many years, my sister and I had a very strained relationship. Being together usually involved a lot of eye rolling and feelings of annoyance. We didn't really like each other that much, frankly. I thought she exaggerated her experience of our parents as kids and she thought I was spoiled and insensitive. Both of these attitudes caused us to be defensive and distrusting of the other. There was usually a time limit before a fight broke out about something from the past we couldn't see eye to eye on. I would swipe a generalization over her like "She should just get over it. We will never have a good relationship." And in that sweeping statement, I was unwittingly wiping away any future hope for us.

It wasn't until I saw my husband's relationship with his brother that I wondered if there wasn't something we could do. He and his brother had just as many issues as my sister and I did but my husband always approached them with understanding and forgiveness rather than eye rolling and exasperation and they had a very good relationship despite their differences. So one day it occurred to me to try to really listen to her without my preconceived filters up. I wanted to truly understand how she felt and what she was angry about. And what I found was that the more I listened to her like a friend and not like the embittered sister role I had fallen into, something profound began to shift between us.

Suddenly, I really did see her side. And I began to feel a genuine compassion for her. My hardened heart of my image of her started to melt. With this, she also began to listen to my side in a way she never had before and understood how I felt. She began to have real compassion for me too. And for the first time in our lives we were speaking to each other like true caring friends. Within a year our relationship had dramatically improved and now I can't even believe how close we have become. Where once I thought we were doomed to become estranged, I now depend on her like a sister should and feel grateful she is in my life. I never in a million years thought this was possible in the rut we were in, but through practicing empathy we made it happen together.

When using the word empathy, it's striking how many people are unfamiliar with the meaning. "Is that like sympathy? Apathy? Homeopathy? What exactly is empathy?" What is striking about this is, if so many people don't know what the word empathy means, how many are incorporating it into their daily lives? Empathy is the ability to recognize and understand the feelings of others. It is the ability to feel what someone else feels, not to only feel for them but to feel with them. Simply put, it's walking a mile in someone else's shoes. It's a lot easier said than done. Why is it so difficult? Does it have something to do with our culture?

A recent study has shown that empathy has dropped almost 50 percent in young people in America since the 1980-1990s, which is quite alarming. Meanwhile, the level of narcissism has increased twofold. Narcissism refers to an inflated view of the self, which tends to sepa-

rate the self from others and to inhibit formation of meaningful relationships. The characteristics of narcissists are such that people focus
on themselves so much that they lose focus on caring about other
people's needs. There are many theories as to why this may be true
but no one seems to be completely sure about the reason.

The Narcissistic Personality Indicator (NPI) was developed in 1970
to assess narcissism and many studies have demonstrated its valid-
ity. Twenge and her colleagues analyzed NPI scores for college students between 1982 and 2007 and found that, over a 25-year period,
the level of narcissism rose significantly and linearly. The level rose
so steadily that by 2007 nearly 70 percent of college students scored
higher in narcissism than the average college student in 1982. What
could be at the crux of this?

The heart of America: survival of the fittest

For many years in America, it has been believed that humans, like nature, are fundamentally selfish, aggressive and competitive. This began at the start of the Industrial Revolution, when probably it was useful to have a picture of humans as competitive and to base the capital
system on that image. The structure of the market economy and the
financial, legal and political lives are all based on this notion, which
essentially pits people against one another. The "gospel of greed" on
Wall Street is just one example that highlights this lack of empathy.
For so long, evolutionary theorists, politicians and the public have focused on competition and the ruthlessness of natural selection as the
way humans are wired that it has essentially built the foundation for
the individualism that defines being an American. Ayn Rand, the famous author whose work is admired by many politicians, champions
the idea that human nature is fundamentally selfish and "man is here
for his own sake".

Whether you believe in this notion or not on the surface, the reality is these beliefs are so ingrained in American culture that most people aren't even aware of it. It permeates everyday life. Competition and being the best are part of what define being American.

Let's think for a moment about the mothers you have met. How many really open up and share what is going on with their kids? How many are really brave enough to be vulnerable and admit they aren't sure if they are doing things right? These days, it seems like fewer and fewer moms are able to be vulnerable as more and more standards are added to the "being a good mother" list of things to live up to and, frankly, compete with other mothers over. Whether it's what you feed your child (organic, breast milk, ecological, etc.), extracurricular activities (how many they are engaged in) or education, there is often a sense of one-upmanship in what should be a normal conversation. And this obviously isn't limited to mothering. It permeates all kinds of discourse. It can be very subtle but if you pay attention, you may be surprised how often you notice it's just under the surface.

Many people feel afraid of really opening up and being vulnerable because they don't want to be judged or rejected. And, in this fear, many relationships get reduced to superficialities.

Our fear of vulnerability and the discovery of the social brain
Brene Brown, a lead researcher in vulnerability, says that people are afraid to be vulnerable because they are actually afraid of disconnection. We so much want social connection that we become afraid to say something that might make another person reject us. And yet, being vulnerable and having empathy are the most connecting things we can practice. So we move from vulnerability to the other side of the spectrum, which is shame. Instead of trying to use empathy and un-

derstand why someone makes the choices they do (not to breastfeed, to breastfeed, to work, not to work—just to name some of the big ones), we shame them. "How can she work and leave her child with strangers? I could never do that! How can she breastfeed so long? It's disgusting! How can she be a housewife? I could never do that! How can she not breastfeed? It's so selfish!" And so it goes on. The broad brush of judgment is swiped across a person and poof! All of your choices become superior and you are obviously a better parent and that feels good. Because being the best is a value we treasure highly. The cruel irony is that we would feel a lot better to have a connected social network where we could feel supported, not judged.

The problem with shaming and striving to be better all the time is that when our own feelings of vulnerability come up, we become very uncomfortable or anxious about how that vulnerability makes us feel. So what do people do when they feel any kind of discomfort or anxiety? The most common reaction is to numb out. Food, TV, shopping, medicine, drugs and alcohol are all good remedies for numbing things out and feeling like everything is ok for those moments. But it is only a band-aid. Yet everyone seems to have a box of these band-aids in their house. In a Ted Talk on vulnerability, Brene Brown says, "We are the most in debt, obese, addicted and medicated society in the world." It makes us ask the question: what if we tried a little more vulnerability and empathy instead of shaming others? What if we stopped aiming for a perfection that doesn't exist? What if we tried to be more connected?

Groundbreaking research in neuroscience has revealed what scientists are calling "the social brain". This is a brain region that lights up when we are engaged in social interactions. Matthew Lieberman, a social cognitive neuroscientist, writes: "This network comes on like a reflex and it directs us to think about other people's minds, their thoughts, feelings and goals. It promotes understanding and empathy, cooperation and consideration." Lieberman believes that we are not only wired for self-interest but also the welfare of others.

The surprise of the Prisoner's Dilemma

To test this, he set up a neuroimaging study of people doing a psychological test called the Prisoner's Dilemma and hooked them up to a functional MRI machine (fMRI) that is used to track blood flow to different parts of the brain. He did this so that he could measure the reactions of the participants' brains during the test.

The background of the setup of the Prisoner's Dilemma is that there are two people and a reward of $10 to be split between them. How much each gets depends on whether the other decides to split things fairly or not. If both players choose to cooperate, each gets $5. If one cooperates but the other chooses to "defect" or pull out, the cooperative player gets nothing and the defector gets all $10. If both defect, they each get $1. The challenge is to decide what to do without knowing what your partner has chosen. Defecting is the safer bet: you'll get at least $1 and possibly $10. If you cooperate, you run the risk that your partner will defect, grabbing the whole pot and leaving you with nothing.

What the results showed was that, contrary to what the researchers thought, the players chose to cooperate more than making the selfish choice of defecting! What could explain this? Moreover, the fMRI results showed that activity in the ventral striatum (the brain's primary reward center) increased as long as both subjects cooperated. And this reward center was more sensitive to the total amount earned by both players rather than to one's own personal outcome. This means that people got more pleasure from the happiness of others than from their own solipsistic happiness! The Danes have always had a fundamental belief that caring about others' happiness is crucial for their own happiness and, judging by these scientific results, they are onto something!

The truth about empathy

Historically, empathy was considered something that separated humans from animals. Most believed that animals and primates didn't exhibit empathy. But the famous primatologist Frans de Waal proves in his book "The Age of Empathy" that empathy is, in fact, visible in all kinds of animals. There are empathy studies now on mice, monkeys, apes, dolphins, elephants, etc., but the general public knows little about it. This is because so many of our governing policies have been based on nature being "a struggle for life" and that we ought to build our societies on competition and selfishness rather than the full spectrum of what it means to be human. From an evolutionary standpoint, empathy was a valuable impulse that helped us survive in groups. Humans could not have survived without empathy and solidarity.

Empathy is the ability to recognize and understand the feelings of others. Simply put, it's walking a mile in someone else's shoes.

Contrary to popular belief, most of us do care about the welfare of others. It has just been lying dormant from lack of focus.

In a study on capuchin monkeys, for example, one monkey could choose between an option that rewarded only himself with food or an option that rewarded himself and a neighbor sitting next to him with food. Guess which one he chose? He chose to give his neighbor food even though it gave him no extra benefit.

People used to think that babies were born without empathy. But that is simply not true. We are all wired for empathy, we just have to learn how to connect the wires to make it work.

Empathy sits in the brain's limbic system. This controls memory, emotions and instinct. It is a complicated neurological system involving mirror neurons and the insula. What many don't realize is that we are biologically predisposed to connect to others. This is made possible through many neuronal systems that are embedded in the right hemisphere of our brain, the mirror neurons being an important aspect of this. The self is not an individual entity, you see, but rather a relational construct.

Daniel Siegel, a clinical professor of psychology at UCLA, says, "Empathy is not a luxury for human beings, it is a necessity. We survive not because we have claws and not because we have big fangs. We survive because we can communicate and collaborate."

Empathy facilitates our connection to others. It develops in infancy through the relationship with the attachment figure. Children first learn to tune into their mother's emotions and moods, and later on with other people. What the mother feels, they will feel and mirror.

This is why things like eye contact, facial expressions and tone of voice are so important in the beginning of life. It is the first way we feel trust and attachment and begin to learn empathy.

Moreover, babies will sometimes soothe other babies with pacifiers or a fluffy toy when they hear them cry. They respond to crying from others being scared or anxious and some even start to cry when they hear it. They may not understand the reason why they are crying or the emotion behind it but this they will learn with time and experience.

Studies show that eighteen-month-old toddlers will almost always try to help an adult who is visibly struggling with a task. If the adult is reaching for something, the toddler will try to hand it to them, or if they see an adult drop something accidentally, they will pick it up. On the other hand, if the same adult throws something to the ground forcefully, they won't pick it up for them. They understand that the action was deliberate and the adult doesn't want it. Even before kids are taught to help or be considerate, perhaps before they understand it's an obligation, children are less selfish than often presumed.

The responsibility of parents
Parents have a big responsibility because they are the primary example of empathy and must practice being empathic themselves. This can be done with their use of language, their behavior and actions. Children will constantly be focused on their parents and will mirror them. Therefore, what they experience in the home will be crucial for their empathy development.

The kinds of families that can quash a child's ability to empathize are the families in which children are exposed to physical, psychological or sexual abuse. They get their borders smashed along with their ability to feel for others. Any child who has suffered an attachment trauma will have their capacity for empathy damaged.

Other types of families that can affect a child's empathy level are the very overprotective ones. These are the parents who are afraid to let their children fail or feel the big emotions and do everything to avoid conflicts and meet their child's slightest wish. These parents sometimes hide their logical, irrational and emotional reactions to "protect" their children. This hinders the child's ability to read others' emotions (and what they see/feel is not what the parents confirm) and this in turn makes them lack empathy. Children from overprotective families, interestingly enough, are the ones who grow up more prone to narcissism, anxiety and depression. They aren't allowed to self-regulate due to the mismatch between feeling and action.

Consequently, the brain development of babies and children who are ignored will be negatively affected by the stress hormone cortisol. And children who are told how to feel and behave all the time will not develop in the same way as those children who are acknowledged and allowed to express their full range of emotions.

Hooking up the wires of empathy in children early on helps them create better, more caring relationships in the future. And we know that it's these caring relationships that are the foundation for true happiness and well-being.

How do the Danes learn to be so empathic?
In the school system in Denmark, there is a mandatory national program implemented as early as preschool called "Step by Step". The children are shown pictures of kids each exhibiting different emotions: sadness, fear, anger, frustration, happiness, etc. The kids talk

about these cards and put into words what the child is sensing and learn to conceptualize their own and others' feelings. They learn to read facial expressions, empathy, problem solving and self-control. The key is that they aren't judgmental of the emotions. It is a way to teach children and young people social skills.

Another program, which is increasingly more popular, is called CAT-kit. The CAT-kit program is used to improve emotional awareness and empathy and focuses on how to articulate experiences, thoughts, feelings and senses. There are many tools in the CAT-kit such as picture cards of faces, measuring sticks to guage intensity of emotions, and pictures of the body where participants can draw on the physical aspects and location of emotions. There is also a tool called "My Circle" where children draw their friends, family members, professionals and strangers in different parts of the circle to help work on understanding others.

The Mary Foundation has had a major impact on empathy training in schools as well. Mary is the Crown Princess, soon to be Queen of Denmark, and she has created an anti-bullying program, which has been implemented across the country. "Free of Bullying" is a program for three-to-eight-year-olds who talk about bullying and teasing and learn to become more caring towards each other. It has yielded positive results and over 98 percent of teachers say they would recommend it to other institutions.

Another less obvious example of empathy training in Danish schools is in how they mix children of different strengths and weaknesses together. Thus, the stronger children academically are put with the less strong ones and the shyer ones with the more gregarious ones and so on. This isn't done so it is a noticeable thing. The teacher gets to know the students with time and then seats them accordingly. The purpose of this is for the students to see that everyone has qualities and to try to help each other. This is related to the zone of proximal development and helping others to reach the next level. The math genius may be great at math but terrible at soccer and vice versa. Seeing that everyone can teach us something if we are open to them is a powerful lesson and it is a very effective teaching tool when students coach each other. This system fosters collaboration and teamwork and to see everyone with respect. Being able to respect and have empathy for others despite having a lot of success is what separates the good from the truly great in the long run.

Some people think that if a child is smart, they should only be with other smart kids. But studies show that there is a huge learning curve in teaching others. Students who teach others work harder to understand material, recall it more precisely and use it more effectively. But they also have to try to understand the difficulties of other students in order to help them where they are having trouble. The ability to explain complicated subject matter to another student is not an easy task but it is an invaluable life skill. Children have to navigate how other kids think and learn and it improves their communication skills dramatically.

"When I was teaching," Iben says, "it was really rewarding to see children discover unexpected strengths in themselves through cooperating and helping others. I could see the results made them happy on a very different level than getting a good grade or being the best at something."

And this comes back to the social brain and what we saw from the fMRI results in the Prisoner's Dilemma. Contrary to what we might think, people's brains actually register more satisfaction from cooperating than from winning alone.

Perhaps then, it is no surprise that empathy is one of the single biggest factors in making successful leaders, entrepreneurs, managers and businesses. It reduces bullying, increases our capacity to forgive and greatly improves relationships and social connectedness. Empathy enhances the quality of meaningful relationships, which we know is one of the most important factors in our sense of well-being. Empathic teenagers are shown to be more successful because they are more purpose driven than their more narcissistic counterparts. And if you think about it, it all makes sense. Successful people don't operate alone; each of us needs the support of others in order to achieve positive results in our lives.

Maybe by focusing on actively teaching empathy to our children as they do in Denmark, we will make happier adults in the future.

The power of words
Knud Ejler Løgstrup, a famous Danish philosopher and theologian who has had a big influence on Danish thought, believed that parents have a responsibility to nourish their children's minds with more than just entertainment and the transfer of knowledge. They should also nourish their ability to empathize. He said that the words we use, or the stories we tell about others, is so important for teaching our children how to be able to put themselves in someone else's place.

When Danes talk about other children in front of their children, for example, it is quite extraordinary to hear the words they use. These words are just cultural language choices. They don't actively think about them. They are simply stock phrases that all parents use to fill space when talking with others. But what is powerful is their tendency to point out the good character qualities in other children. It is very common to hear "He is such a sweet boy isn't he?", "She is very kind don't you think?", "That was very helpful of him, didn't you think so?", "He is nice. Do you think so?"

What is remarkable about this is to think how these word choices are laying the groundwork for seeing the good in others as a default setting in the future. By pointing out the good in others, it becomes natural to see the good in others. It becomes more natural to trust. It is rare indeed to hear a Danish person talking negatively about another child in front of their children.

What they do instead is try to explain the behavior of others and why they might have acted in an unpleasant way. "She was probably very tired and missed her nap." "Do you think he was hungry? You know how grumpy we can be when we are hungry." They try to lead their children to seeing a child's behavior as merely affected by a circumstance rather than labeling them as mean, selfish or obnoxious. This is the supporting language we talked about in Reframing.

And, in fact, this is really how the ability of reframing begins. Being able to easily imagine that someone might be having a hard time makes us much more able to see their behavior in an understanding light. Instead of swiping a broad brush of a negative label, we can lighten our perspective with empathy. This unwittingly makes us feel better because it saves a lot of time on negative energy.

The philosopher Løgstrup wasn't being naïve to think that trusting in others would always be rewarded. He merely believed that trust, like other "sovereign expressions of life" such as speech openness, love and compassion, was fundamental in man. "To show confidence and trust in others is to deliver oneself." And it's true. Trusting is very freeing.

The Danish Way of teaching empathy
One of the first things to consider in terms of teaching empathy is to distinguish between the capacity for empathy and the consequences: i.e., how one should put empathy into action in relation to others. This must be learned and it takes a long time and a lot of good examples from parents and others who are with children on a daily basis.

Empathy is one of the single biggest factors in making successful leaders, entrepreneurs, managers and businesses. It reduces bullying, increases our capacity to forgive and greatly improves relationships and social connectedness.

Let us give you an example:

Lisa is playing by the sea with a shovel and Mark, a younger child, wants to play with it, but Lisa refuses. Mark starts crying. What should Lisa do? What many parents would do is give the shovel to Mark because he is crying. But what does this teach? Is it true that we have to always give someone what they want because they want it? This is, again, teaching how to do things because there is an extrinsic consequence rather than an internal rationalizing. Lisa plays with the shovel and she can sense Mark is getting upset. She needs an adult to help her balance her own needs and limits, and then make a decision that she can vouch for and take responsibility for herself. What often happens in these kinds of conflicts is the adults will have compassion for Mark and demand that Lisa lives the adult's compassion, forcing her to give Mark the shovel. This is neither fair, nor empathic. This doesn't mean that Lisa shouldn't learn to take into account others' feelings (not at all) but what is important is to teach children that parents have empathy and compassion for them as well (understanding how they feel and their needs), which will give them the tools to truly use it themselves. It also teaches Mark that he does not necessarily achieve anything by crying.

In the long term, these kinds of lessons in empathy can be huge. When you teach a child that they aren't forced to do something to appease another just to make things easier, it transfers over into a powerful lesson in the long run. Teenagers who get around the wrong kind of peer pressure will have an easier time standing for what they feel is right if they have been shown that their feelings are valid from early on. A fourteen-year-old who is pressured to have sex with her boyfriend, for example, may be afraid to say no because she is afraid of upsetting him. But she will know that just because her boyfriend wants her to give him something she doesn't feel is right, she doesn't have to. It's like her brother crying over the shovel on the beach. Her parents taught her how to handle the situation with empathy and fairness. She will teach her boyfriend to respect her feelings, like she had been taught to respect herself and others by her own parents. If we raise our kids with empathy, they will have a much easier time understanding and practicing it themselves. When their internal compass is strong, it leads them the right way.

Something Danes do a lot with their kids is pointing out the emotions of others. Perhaps this comes from the training they get early on in school along with it being a learned default setting from their parents.

"Aw, can you see Victor is crying?"
"Why do you think he is crying?"
"She looks angry."
"Why do you think she is angry?"
"I can see you are upset."
"Can you try to tell me why?"

It's very rare to hear anyone responding with:

"Don't be like that. There is no reason to be angry."
"Why is she angry, that is ridiculous!"
"You have nothing to cry about, stop crying!"
"Why are you upset?"
"You should be happy!"

They will always at least acknowledge the emotion before discussing it with the child. "Oh? Why are you crying?" and they get down on their level to show them they see them.
"I see you are upset. What are you upset about?"

"Because she took your toy?"

"She is just a little baby. I don't think she did it on purpose, do you?"

There aren't always good reasons for a child's emotions or easy solutions to them but by at least acknowledging them and trying not to judge them, we are teaching respect. Imagine if we as adults were constantly disregarded for our emotional states as being ridiculous, unnecessary or wrong and told how to feel instead?

One of the main pillars in the Danish Way of teaching empathy is not judging. Danes try not to judge their children, their friends, their children's friends or their family too harshly. All members of a family have a right to be heard and taken seriously, not just the one who screams the loudest. Being tolerant of yourself and others is paramount.

And remember, by embedding a more empathic, less shaming and more vulnerable, authentic style into your household, your children will grow up to be less judgmental of you in the long run. That is just food for thought.

Parents have a big responsibility because they are the primary example of empathy and must practice being empathic themselves.

TIPS FOR EMPATHY

How can we put the Danish Way of empathy into practice?

1. FIGURE OUT YOUR OWN EMPATHIC STYLE

It starts with you and your partner.

Some questions to ask and discuss are

1. What does empathy mean for me?
2. What does empathy mean for my partner?
3. Where do we agree and disagree?
4. What are our values to the core?
5. How judgmental am I of myself and others? How judgmental is my partner of others?
6. How does our language style reflect this?
7. How can I change my language style so as to reflect a more empathic style with less judgment? (Remember, this isn't easy but with practice you get better. Try listening to yourself first to see how much you talk about others and then think of alternate ways to express yourself that involve more empathy. Remember, your children are mirroring you.) Help your partner do the same.

2. UNDERSTAND OTHERS

Practice understanding others instead of shaming them. You will be amazed how often this is happening and what a difference it makes to find a reason to defend others by putting yourself in their shoes. This is really putting empathy into practice.

3. EXPERIENCING EMOTIONS

Help your child see others' emotions as well as experiencing their own without putting on your own judgment. "Sally was angry? Why was she angry? What happened? What do you think about what happened?" Not "She shouldn't have been angry and done that."

4. READ, READ, READ

Studies show that reading to your children markedly increases their empathy levels. And not just reading nice books but reading books that encompass all emotions, including bad and uncomfortable ones. When my husband used to bring home Danish books for the kids, I was appalled. They dealt with issues I thought were inappropriate and, "gasp", didn't have a happy ending! But I realized that we were giving our kids a gift by exposing them to the whole range of emotions and talking about them. Dealing with reality, even at the level they can handle, is honest and authentic and is proven to significantly improve empathy.

5. IMPROVE MEANINGFUL RELATIONSHIPS

Try using empathy to patch up some of your own relationships. Having fractured relationships has been proven to cause physical and psychological damage. Empathy and forgiveness activate the same region of the brain, which means the more you hone your empathy skills, the easier it is to forgive and be forgiven. Meaningful friend and family relationships are the top factors in true happiness, well above having a lot of money.

6. BE VULNERABLE

Try to be a better listener and don't be afraid to be vulnerable. It's the most connecting thing we can do. Listen, be curious, mirror and use metaphors for showing that you provide caring responses.

7. THE DANISH WAY

Surround yourself with others who want to practice the Danish Way. New mothers and parents are the ones who can benefit enormously from this support.

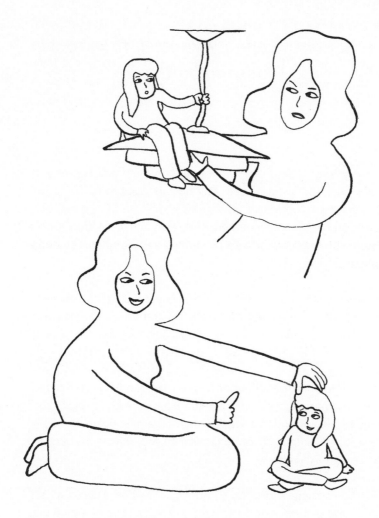

No Ultimatums

"It is better to conquer yourself than to win a thousand battles."

BUDDHA

We have all seen it before or have been there before ourselves with our own children. We are tired, our kids are disobeying or not listening and despite our best efforts, they continue to misbehave or annoy us and we snap. Some people scream and yell, some people threaten with timeouts or take something away, and some people use physicality.

I have seen numerous friends and fellow parents yell at or spank their children. It often comes from the frustration of their child not listening to an ultimatum. The scene usually goes like this: "You'd better do that right now or else!" or "If you don't stop that right now, you're going to get it... I mean it!" "If I ask you one more time, that's it!" And once the ultimatum is out there, and all resources exhausted, the parents feel they have to follow through to regain control and the result ends up in spanking, screaming or physicality of some sort. If this doesn't sound familiar to you, maybe it's because it isn't being talked about.

Some studies suggest that up to 80-90 percent of Americans still use spanking as a form of discipline for their children. I myself was spanked as a child as was my sister. I don't blame my parents for spanking us. I know they were just operating off of their own default settings from their upbringing, which had been quite physical. For a long time, I never questioned spanking as a way of disciplining. When I was in elementary school, corporal punishment had only recently been abolished. I thought it was completely normal and never felt I'd had a problem with it.

It wasn't until I was pregnant with my first child that I realized how different my husband's outlook on disciplining was from mine. Our discussions on the subject began to make me consider another way of educating our kids than what would have probably become my natural default setting. And the journey to this discovery has been eye-opening.

Upon researching for the book, we learned that there are currently 19 states in the US where corporal punishment is still allowed in schools. That is, hitting students with a paddle or a cane for misbehaving. Although corporal punishment in schools has been banned in 31 states, it is still allowed in private schools in 50 states. This may or may not come as a surprise to you. The point is: spanking is still very prevalent.

In fact, a large-scale study conducted by the Centers for Disease Control (CDC) viewing parenting practices across the US confirms that we use physicality more than one might think. The study, which measured five different culture groups across America (Asian, Hispanic, African-American, non-Hispanic whites and American Indian) composed of 240 focus groups in 6 different cities across the US, found that all of the groups claimed, at some time or another, to use physical punishment when necessary.

What was even more striking were the differences across cultures in terms of when and where they spanked. African-American mothers, for example, said they spanked right away. One woman said, "Don't get mad and whip them for everything they did two weeks ago. You have to nip it in the bud." White and American Indian parents, conversely, were uncomfortable spanking in public. In a restaurant (a situation that came up often in the discussions), white parents often talked about taking the child into the bathroom for spanking, while American Indian parents preferred to delay it until they got home. This just illustrates that more spanking may be happening behind closed doors.

The four types of parenting styles

There are four different types of parenting styles as defined by developmental psychologists.

Authoritarian: These parents are demanding but not responsive. They want obedience and have high standards, the classic tiger mom. Children of authoritarian parents tend to do well in school but sometimes suffer from low self-esteem, depression and poor social skills.

Authoritative: (not to be confused with authoritarian) These parents are demanding but responsive. They set high standards as well but are supportive in their discipline. Children of authoritative parents are rated more socially and intellectually competent than those of other parents.

Permissive: Highly responsive but seldom demand mature behavior from their child, depending instead on self-regulation from the child. Children of permissive parents tend to have problems in school and with their behavior.

Uninvolved: These parents are neither responsive nor demanding, but not to the point of being neglectful. Children of uninvolved parents do most poorly in all areas.

Authoritarian parents are described as being low in responsiveness and high in control. A response to a child being raised by authoritarian parents would be "Because I said so." Children aren't encouraged to ask why. They are encouraged to do as they are told.

Some of the challenges associated with authoritarian parenting are that being very controlling can make kids rebel. Second, not offering much support apart from "Because I said so," "Pull up your socks," "Straighten up," or "It's my way or the highway," leaves kids on their own to regulate their emotions, which, when coupled with fear and shame, can be confusing and upsetting.

Authoritarian parents typically parent this way because they were raised like that themselves and feel they turned out fine. Since most people don't want to blame their parents for spanking, lest they suggest some kind of scarring, instead say "I probably got what I deserved." Or "I turned out just fine." And maybe they did. But if someone says they smoked their whole life and turned out ok, does that mean smoking is good for us?

The hard truth about spanking
A recent analysis covering two decades' worth of research on the long-term effects of physical punishment on children concludes that spanking not only doesn't work, but it can actually wreak havoc on kids' long-term development.

The study found that regardless of the age of the child or the sample size of the children, not one of more than 80 studies succeeded in finding any positive associations with physical punishment. Not one. What associations it did find were these: children who are spanked may feel depressed and devalued. Their sense of self-worth can suffer. Harsh punishments can wind up backfiring because they can foster lying in children who are desperate to avoid being spanked. Later in life, physical punishment is linked to mental health problems including depression, anxiety and drug and alcohol use. There's neuroimaging evidence that physical punishment may alter parts of the brain involved in performance on IQ tests and up the likelihood of substance abuse. And there is also data that supports that spanking can affect areas of the brain involved in emotion and stress regulation.

Parents spank because they think it is effective. And maybe it is, in the short term. But beyond that, it becomes pretty ineffective. Kids learn to listen because they are afraid. Power struggles create distance and hostility instead of closeness and trust. Distance and hostility create resentment, resistance and rebellion (or compliance with lowered self-esteem). And where do you go after hitting them if they continue the bad behavior? Hit them harder? Scream louder? Beat them into compliance? Not surprisingly, one of the most common long-term consequences of spanking is aggression.

Case in point: one mother in a spanking study conducted by parenting expert George Holden hit her toddler after the toddler either hit or kicked her mother, saying, "This is to help you remember not to hit your mother." "The irony is just amazing," says Holden. And let's not mention how many of us go on to repeat the habit unintentionally as parents. But do we ever ask the question, "Is incessant yelling or spanking really necessary?" The reality is that many of us don't ask that question until it is too late.

What are the world's happiest people's thoughts on spanking, screaming and power struggles?

In Denmark, spanking became illegal in 1984. Most Danes think it is extremely strange, almost unthinkable, to consider using spanking as a form of disciplining for a child. In Sweden, it was actually abolished earlier in 1979. And now more than 32 countries, much of Europe, Costa Rica, Israel, Tunisia and Kenya, have similar laws, to name a few.

The parenting style used in Denmark is very democratic. It is most closely related to the authoritative style. That is, they establish rules and guidelines that their children are expected to follow. However, they are very responsive to their children's questions about the rules. They see children as intrinsically good and react to them accordingly. For example, an interesting difference in language between Danish and English is how we call the toddler years. In English it is called the "terrible twos", whereas in Danish it is called "trodsalder" (the boundary age); children pushing boundaries is normal and welcomed, not annoying and terrible. When you see it that way, it is easier to welcome the misbehavior rather than seeing it as bad and deserving of punishment.

As for screaming and shouting at their kids, you will rarely hear this in Denmark. Households full of yelling is an extremely uncommon occurrence indeed. How do they do it? One of the parents we interviewed summed it up pretty well. She said, "First and foremost, I think we must remain calm as parents and try not to lose control of ourselves. For how can we expect our kids to control themselves if we can't do it? That seems unfair."

This doesn't mean the Danes are soft or weak, not at all, but firmness and kindness can replace losing your temper and going into immediate power struggles and ultimatums. Avoiding these makes for a more peaceful and safer-feeling atmosphere.

In Denmark, spanking became illegal in 1984. Most Danes think it is extremely strange, almost unthinkable, to consider using spanking as a form of disciplining for a child.

Parenting with respect

The Danes want their children to be respectful absolutely, but respect goes both ways. You have to give it to receive it. Governing with fear is a problem, because it doesn't foster respect, it fosters fear. There is a difference between firmness and fear. With fear, the child won't always know the real reason they shouldn't do something, they merely want to avoid being hurt or yelled at. This doesn't facilitate a strong sense of core self. A strong sense of core self comes from questioning and understanding what rules are, why they exist and then truly incorporating them and valuing them. Being afraid of something called a rule is something very different. Living in a hostile environment of yelling doesn't help either. And likewise, you won't know if your child is being honest with you in the future if they are afraid of you. They may tell you what they think you want to hear out of fear. Fear is powerful but not conducive to an atmosphere of closeness and trust. You will have a much more positive influence and a genuinely closer relationship in an atmosphere of respect and calmness where there is no fear of blame, shame or pain.

In fact, studies show that children from authoritative parents are more likely to become self-reliant, socially accepted, academically successful and well-behaved. They are less likely to report depression and anxiety, and less likely to engage in antisocial behavior like delinquency and drug use. Research suggests that having even one authoritative parent can make a huge difference. They are also more attuned to their parents and less influenced by their peers. In a study of American students, undergraduates were presented with a series of moral problems and asked how they would solve them. Students from authoritative families were more likely than others to say that their parents, not their peers, would influence their decisions.

How the Danes practice no ultimatums in school

One of the ways they promote democracy in Danish schools is by allowing students to create the rules together with their teacher every year. At the beginning of school, teachers talk with their students at length about what it means to have a good class and what values and behaviors they think they should implement to make it a good class. The rules can be anything from being on time to not interrupting to being respectful of others. But what is important is that everyone decides the code of conduct together. No set of rules for any class is the same. And they do this every year because the students are older and more mature and have different senses of responsibility than in the previous years. This system helps regulate class behavior because students feel a sense of responsibility towards each other since they decided the rules together.

"I saw this a lot in the years I was teaching," Iben says. "In my daughter Julie's class this year, for instance, if someone is being too loud or interrupting, the whole class has to stand up and walk around the class and clap their hands 10 times. This was something they all decided at the beginning of the year. So the kids who are being too loud feel a direct responsibility and effect on their peers, not just on the teacher. This can be a surprisingly powerful motivator to stop."

In Denmark, they devote a lot more time and energy on how to avoid problems rather than on how to punish them. Most Danish schools are supplied with different kinds of equipment to deal with various issues students may have. For instance, children who suffer from ADHD or hyperactivity can sit on something called a ball cushion, which helps them concentrate in class. The ball cushion is an inflatable cushion with spiky massage nobs on one side. Used to promote good back health, it stimulates the postural muscles to sit up straighter and keep balance. The body senses a shift in gravity, which sends an impulse to sit up straight and this unconsciously increases concentration. Iben's daughter's class has three kids who are sitting on ball cushions this year.

Schools are also provided with "fidget sets" and "cuddle things" for kids who have a hard time sitting still and not fidgeting, which can lead to disturbing others. Inside these sets are things like stress balls and spaghetti-like strings they can busy their hands with, which inadvertently helps them pay attention and focus. For kids who are really too full of energy or aggressive, they may be asked to run laps to help them burn off some of the excess energy.

A guiding principle that teachers are trained to follow in Danish schools is called "differentiere". This basically means that teachers learn to see each student as an individual with specific needs. They make goal plans together with every student and follow up on their growth twice a year. The objectives can be academic, personal as well as social. The idea is that by "differentiating" the students, it helps the teacher understand their individual needs better so they can act and react accordingly.

This is important because, as we have seen in the previous chapters, how you choose to see children makes a big difference in your reaction to them. If you see them as naughty and manipulative, you will react accordingly. If you see them as innocent and doing exactly what they are programmed to do, you are much more likely to react by nurturing and forgiving them, even helping them rather than punishing them. Patience is much more easily summoned when one sees the harmless intentions and goodness in an otherwise annoy-ing child. This is a cycle that comes back to you. Good begets good. Calm begets calm. Remember, it isn't the child who is bad. It is the action that is bad. It is always important to separate that.

Avoiding power struggles

Iben gives an example of how she avoided power struggles with a student when she was teaching. "There was this boy who was very provocative and rebellious in my class. He was getting the label of being a troublemaker. A lot of the students probably thought I was too easy on him but I felt it was very important to stay away from framing him as a bad kid and having a lot of conflict with him. I knew he had a difficult home life and I always saw him as a sweet, loving boy. He was funny and clever and I focused on the strengths in him, and chose to ignore the rest so as not to thicken the bad storyline about himself. I spoke to him with respect and I trusted in his abili-ties to come out as a good person. Many years later he came to a school reunion despite having bad memories of the place. He had completely turned his life around and had come to say thank you. He remembered me telling him that I wasn't worried about him and that I knew he would do well in life. He said that the trust I'd had for him had given him the strength to trust in himself and become a better person. I was so touched I cried! It was then that I realized how important separating the behavior from the person truly was. By trusting and helping people reframe themselves, and treating the behavior as the behavior and not the child, helps build a more loving storyline of one's life. It also helps avoid conflict."

So now we have seen why a more democratic approach is clearly beneficial for the well-being, happiness and resilience of our children. How can we put the Danish Way of no ultimatums into practice?

Put a mirror up to yourself

Think of the things you most dislike hearing in yourself and then put a mirror up. That is what you will get from your child. If you don't like the yelling and the hands going up in exasperation, don't do it. If you don't like physicality, don't do it.

Stop worrying about what others think

Stop worrying about what others think of you or your child's behavior. Yelling and physicality often come from the added stress of someone watching you. Whether you are at a friend's house or with your family or out in a restaurant or shop, keep your behavior in line with your values. It's about being authentic and behaving in accordance with what you believe. Don't worry about how others raise their kids or how your family thinks you should raise yours. Focus on doing what is right for your children and believe in that success. Most people just repeat their own patterns. You are doing something much bigger and harder by making a change. Try forming a group of parents who share the same values as you within the Danish Way and support each other. Believe in your values and stand by what you are fighting for. The proof is in the pudding for raising happier, more resilient and better-adjusted adults.

The Danish Way does work. If you feel torn about a power struggle over eating or being polite or belligerent in front of friends or family, don't go there. Breathe, remain calm, think. Use humor. Offer a way out. Don't worry how a friend might or might not judge you or your kids. Your kids, in the long run, will be happier and healthier and that is what matters.

Chill out and remember the big lines

Know the difference between the battles and the war and don't take every battle. Is it really important that their clothes or hair look perfect all the time? Is it really important that they don't wear that Batman shirt one more day? Is it really important that they clean their plate right now because you said so? Or they try spinach because they need to right now? Is it really worth it? This is what you have to decipher and decide with your partner when the big lines need to be enforced. Maybe at a friend's house or out at dinner isn't the right time. What are your big lines and when do you really want to try to educate and enforce those big lines? Keep in mind that if you make a scene in public, is it really being respectful to you and your child? You have to be consistent but you don't have to raise soldiers. Remember kids go through phases when they don't want to do/eat/wear/say things. They grow out of them. If you are consistent with the big lines, they will understand them. The key is to have patience and the wherewithal to get through those phases without losing your cool and staying focused on what is important.

Don't worry about how others raise their kids or how your family thinks you should raise yours. Focus on doing what is right for your children and believe in that success

My daughter refused to wear a jacket or socks for some time. It was very frustrating and nothing worked except taking her outside with no jacket or socks and she realized, "Hey, I am cold, put that on!" It was frustrating and it took more time in the mornings but she grew out of it. She didn't say hello to people for a while either. People stopped and said hello and she looked away. I kept insisting but I never forced it. One day, 6 months later, she started saying hello unprompted and always did from there on in. She ate vegetables as a little kid and then stopped eating them all of a sudden. She only wanted white pasta. I never made a thing about it. I just offered different foods on the table and mentioned it was funny that she used to love vegetables. Now she eats them again. She got over making a thing about it. Kids are testing things for themselves as well. If it becomes too much of a power game everyone loses and life becomes more unpleasant than it needs to be. If you stay cool, so will they.

Examples of no ultimatums—offering a way out
The child is throwing something you don't want them to.
Typical response: "Don't throw that! If you throw that one more time, that's it!"

Option: take it away. Distract. Remove the child. Use humor. When you say no, be calm about it. Show them what throwing it can do. Mime an "ow ow" from being hit by the object and give it back. If they throw it again, show them again, shaking your head looking distressed. "Ow, ow!" They may not get it the first time, but over time they will and will understand more.

Hitting or biting others is unacceptable and in those cases, we should be firm and hold them and tell them "No!" forcefully and make them look at you and give you an apology sound and a ca-ress so they learn the meaning of sorry early on and the non-use of physicality. Remember this happens fast because children forget in an instant what they did. You have to deal with that directly in the moment. They may not understand what the meaning of sorry is in the beginning, but with time and learning to empathize they will.

Dinnertime is a big place for power struggles

A child's reaction to food is often about how hungry they are. If they have eaten too much in the afternoon, for example, then they are probably not very hungry. Or they may be so hungry that they need to regulate their blood sugar to feel better. Eating to regulate their blood sugar will surely affect how they are acting. Using empathy will help you to understand where they are coming from and react accordingly. Being understanding rather than angry is a good place to start. Imagine how you would feel in either situation if you were over-hungry or full and go from there.

Something to keep in mind: teaching a child to enjoy and respect food is a great gift. Food is what sustains us and having a healthy, loving relationship to it can create a lifetime of happiness. Check your own relationship to food and make sure yours is as healthy as it can be. Mealtimes, above all, should be an enjoyable place for the family to come together.

It's our responsibility as parents to put ample food on the table. Put a little of everything on your children's plates and let them eat their food as they wish. Food situations should be nice and cozy above all, not marked by tension and focused on the fact that they have to eat. Most people would lose their appetite under these conditions!

If children refuse to eat, try making a deal with them. If they eat a little of their beans or their meat, they can have a yogurt for dessert. Take out the bites you want them to eat. It doesn't have to be many but enough so that there is some negotiation. If they really won't eat and it becomes unpleasant, don't force it.

If you make it a big deal, it will be a big deal. The food is there. If they want it, they can come back for it. We don't always love the food we are served or clear our plates or force ourselves to try things we don't like. Sometimes we do but not always. Give them a way out when you can, win/win. They will have more respect for you when they discover a rule for themselves. Always keep in mind that you are the example.

Low stress makes everything uncharged. Especially food. Remember, there are phases for your children with food as well. Giving healthy choices with food on the table, cutting out unhealthy snacks and making mealtimes pleasurable and not a prison camp will teach your child that food is a lovely, enjoyable thing.

A phrase used a lot in Denmark to encourage kids to eat is, "You have to eat this food so you can be big and strong! Do you want to be big and strong?" They make the child flex their muscles to show how strong they are and assure them that it comes from the vegetables and healthy foods they are eating. It works more often than you might think!

Explain the rules and ask for understanding
"Put your seatbelt on."
"No, I don't want to."
"Do you remember why I told you to buckle your seatbelt?"
"No."

"Because if we have an accident you could be very hurt and have to go to the hospital. Do you want to go to the hospital?"

"No."

(Put the seatbelt on firmly)

If they continue to balk, you go more into what it is to be hurt and if they like to be hurt. They won't be. You reiterate that a seatbelt is to prevent them from being hurt. The more you explain things in ways that they can understand, the better. You know your own child and which line of reasoning will make most sense.

Getting started

1. Make an action plan. What are your values with regard to your children? Include both your own and your partner's.
2. Are you spanking or hitting? Make a vow to stop. It isn't necessary and it doesn't foster trust and respect.
3. Are you yelling too much? Make a vow to stop. Use it only when necessary. Yelling isn't pleasant for anyone. Your children mirror you. You are their role model. If you want them to control themselves and behave, then you have to set the example of controlling yourself.

How can we avoid spanking and yelling? Find ways to reduce your own stress. Get more sleep. Breathe. Exercise more. Get some time away. Yelling and hitting often come from a lack of surplus time for yourself to process and have the space between your reactions to choose your response better.

If you feel yourself close to exploding or yelling, take a deep breath. Go into another room and give yourself a timeout. If you can pass the baton to your partner, do it. Try to be aligned in your values of no hitting and yelling and always form a strong front on what you do or don't want your kids to be doing. This alliance is crucial. It also helps because you can more easily keep each other in check on your outbursts. So if one of you is at your limit and ready to break, then calmly ask the other to take over. Within a short period of time, you will begin to see your children behaving more calmly as a result.

How can we practice the Danish Way of no ultimatums?

1. BAD PARENTING

There aren't bad children, there is bad parenting.

2. POWER STRUGGLES

If you don't look for power struggles, you won't find them. Always think win/win, not how can I win.

3. DON'T BLAME THEM

Blame yourself and try to be better.

4. CHILDREN ARE INHERENTLY GOOD

Always see your children as inherently good. They are supposed to push boundaries and test the rules. They are not bad and manipulative. This is how they grow.

5. TEACH THEM

Guide them, nurture them and educate them. Don't just punish them and see them as needing more discipline. Try finding ways to manage difficult behaviors. Don't bestow words upon them such as "sneaky" and "manipulative" and "terrible." These labels do matter. The behavior is the behavior, not the child.

6. REFRAME

Find the better storyline about your children and other people. Reframe. Learning how to reframe and teaching your children to do it makes everyone happier.

7. REMEMBER: THE CYCLE COMES BACK TO YOU

Good begets good. Bad begets bad. Out of control begets out of control and calm begets calm.

8. GET YOUR PARTNER IN ON THIS

Remember, research shows that even one parent following this style and keeping their cool can make a big difference.

9. WRITE DOWN YOUR ULTIMATUMS

Write down all the ultimatums you use on a regular basis. How are those comparable to the ones your parents used? How can we turn those into something more positive?

10. ALWAYS THINK OF YOUR CHILD'S AGE

What can you expect from your child in relation to his or her age (zone of proximal development)? Every age has a "theme" of what can be expected from it.

11. BE ACCEPTING OF ALL KINDS OF FEELINGS

Accept your child's feelings whether they are in the mood you want them to be in or not. It doesn't matter what other people think of your child's mood. Sometimes everyone has a bad day, even kids. By not stressing over it, you draw less attention to it and it's more respectful of their own abilities to self-regulate.

12. PROTEST IS A RESPONSE TO SOMETHING

Remember that "protest" can also be a sign of independence to be launched to develop independence. Appreciate it for what it is, not only a terrible annoyance. They are growing.

13. PUT THE BAD BEHAVIOR IN CONTEXT

Have there been any changes in your child's life that may affect behavioral change?

14. WHAT MAKES YOU SNAP

It's important to know what makes you snap. Where is your breaking point and what can you do when you get there to stop yourself? Do you need more sleep, some downtime or exercise? Listen to your needs and ask for help.

15. SHOW THAT YOU LISTEN

Make sure that you show your child that you listen to them. For example, when they ask for something, it is important to show them that it is heard and understood—even if it cannot be done. Repeat it back to them so they know you heard. "I can hear that you would like a lollipop but..." Explain to your child why something can be done/not done. Teach respect, be respectful and you will be more respected.

Togetherness and Hygge

"Good teams become great ones, when the members trust each other enough to surrender the 'me' for the 'we'."

PHIL JACKSON

When I first met my husband's family and spent time with them 13 years ago, the experience was a little overwhelming to say the least. "At hygge sig" or "hygge" (pronounced hooga), which literally means "to cozy around together", was a way of life for them. Cozying around together involved lighting candles, playing games together, eating nice meals, having cake and tea, and just generally being in each other's company in a "cozy" atmosphere. This very large family would come together for days on end to just "cozy around" without much of a break from each other. I found this group gathering a little odd in the beginning, but after 13 years of studying the phenomenon, we have finally worked out what the secret to hygge is.

You see, my family was very different. We, as a rule, could only be around each other for limited amounts of time, after which we would need a break from each other. We did this respectfully but also knowing that having breaks and doing our own thing was just a part of our way of life. Feeling the need to "cozy around" together for unbroken amounts of time would have almost seemed like an infringement on our individual rights as Americans. It also sounded like a recipe for disaster to argue about something. In fact, I couldn't understand how the Danish families seemed able to "cozy around" together so long without more family drama. Surely, with siblings and relatives around, someone had to have problems, issues or at the very least a neurotic tendency to gossip about? There seemed to be very little negativity, no complaining and despite the number of people gathered, they operated together like a well-oiled machine. What in the world was going on?

Could this cozy togetherness time be part of the reason the Danes are so consistently voted as the happiest people in the world? The answer is an absolute yes!

Research shows that one of the number one predictors of well-being and happiness is quality time with friends and family. Our modern world doesn't always allow for this but the Danish Way incorporates "hygge" into everyday life to guarantee it.

Hygge as a way of life
The word "hygge" dates back to the 19th century. It is derived from the Germanic word "hyggja", which means to think or feel satisfied. It is comfort and it is both an identity-related symbol and a mood to be in. There are even moral meanings attached to hygge. For example, hygge is something Danes identify with both in action and in being. A holiday such as Christmas, for example, is centered on this. Christmas is a time when the family gets together from near and far and therefore comfort or "hygge" is indispensable.

Because Danes see hygge as a way of life, they all try to make it happen. That is, a cozy time together with family and friends. So, at

Christmas, they all work together to make sure there is maximum comfort. It is a team effort. This includes things like making the atmosphere very nice with candles and nice food, but also in their way of being. They try to help out so that one person or a few don't feel like the only ones doing the work. Children are encouraged to play with and help the younger ones. They try to engage in games that everyone can take part in and they all make an effort to play them even if they don't particularly want to. That wouldn't be "hyggeligt" or it would be "not cozy". They try to leave their personal problems behind for those times and be positive and stay away from too much discord because they value this cozy time together and want it to be just that. There are lots of other times to worry about our lives and our stressors but happiness also comes from setting those times aside and being in the moment with the ones we love. Having a warm and lovely experience together for the Danes is the ultimate end goal and it is a great example to pass on to our children.

Feeling connected to others gives meaning and purpose to all of our lives and this is why the Danes value hygge so highly. The individual is prized absolutely but without the interaction and support of others they don't think that they can be truly happy as a whole person. In Denmark, cozying around and togetherness are part of their cultural foundation.

The American bedrock
This idea of togetherness, if you think about it, is quite different from the individualistic nature that forms a large piece of the American bedrock. America was built on the philosophy of self-reliance. We don't really need others if we are strong enough to succeed on our own. Why should we have to depend on support if we can do it ourselves? We glorify individual achievement and self-fulfillment

with terms like "the self-made man" and the individual hero in all walks of life from political to social to sports. If you listen to sports, it is rarely about the team effort but rather the individual who shines out: the famous quarterback or the pitcher. It's the star who shines out from the rest. The people who help support that star often become blurred background noise. It's the hard worker and the survival of the fittest we admire most. We are then raised to strive to be that star, to be that winner. Geert Hofstede, a world-renowned cultural psychologist, concluded in a very famous study about cultural differences that America had the highest level of individualism in the world. That is pretty incredible. We are so programmed to think about "I" that we probably don't even realize it.

The word "hygge" dates back to the 19th century. It is derived from the Germanic word "hyggja", which means to think or feel satisfied. It is comfort and it is both an identity-related symbol and a mood to be in.

This is not in any way saying that America doesn't have an incredibly strong community spirit, not at all. It is merely pointing out that, culturally speaking, we are more programmed to think individualistically. During a family gathering, for example, it is a lot more normal to think about how "I" feel rather than how "we" feel. We talk about things like "me time" or meeting "my needs" or figuring out how it makes "me" feel rather than "we" feel.

Moreover, it's fair to say that most of us would enjoy being "a winner". We would like our kids to be winners or at the very least to be the best at something and stand out. This is pretty normal. Who wouldn't want that? Just look at the number of awards given out in schools these days for a creative myriad of reasons. Whether it is for the silliest joke, the sweetest smile or the best jump roper in class, we all strive to win something. It's woven into the very fabric of our culture.

Alternatively, how many of us would naturally consider giving the winning trophy for "the harmony of the group?" How many of us would gauge our child's success, not on how well they played, but rather on how well they helped others play or on how well they played together?

When you substitute the "I" for the "we" even illness becomes wellness

The concept of togetherness and hygge has so many implications but essentially it is putting yourself aside for the benefit of the whole. Leaving the drama at the door and sacrificing your own individual needs and desires to make a group gathering more pleasant. This is a much nicer experience to pass on to your children. They don't enjoy adult drama, negativity and divisiveness. Kids are very happy to be together and cozy around! By learning to hygge, they will be able to pass this on to their kids.

There is a famous fable about heaven and hell we felt illustrated this concept well. In hell, there is a long table with a glorious feast of wine and food and candles but the feeling is cold. The people around the table are pale and emaciated and there is a cacophony of wails and cries filling the room. Instead of arms, they have very long sticks for arms, which is preventing them from getting the food to their mouths. Try as they might, it is futile. They are all starving despite the rich bounty of food in front of them.

In heaven, however, there is much the same scene. There is still the long table and the feast and the candles but here the table is surrounded by jovial, laughing people. They are singing and eating. The atmosphere is warm and lively and everyone is enjoying the food and the wine and the company. The irony is, they too have very long sticks for arms. The only difference is, instead of trying to feed themselves, they are feeding each other. A change in perspective has turned hell into heaven—a simple metaphor to illustrate how substituting the "me" for the "we" can have dramatic results.

Teamwork in Denmark
In Denmark from very early on, children work on group projects to encourage them to learn to help others and engage in teamwork and team building. They try to teach them to seek out others' strengths and weaknesses and see how they can help others. Children are taught to find the good qualities and the potential even where it is sometimes unexpected. They encourage humility in their star pupils. They want their children to be empathic and care about others. Only caring about yourself isn't "hyggeligt". We also saw this

in Empathy how teachers put pupils of different strengths and weaknesses together. This facilitates cooperation with all kinds of different people, which becomes an invaluable skill as an adult.

Something else they have that is huge in Denmark is called "foreningsliv" or "association life". These associations or social groups are built on voluntary participation and the interaction of individuals who work in partnership on an interest. The objective can be economic, political, academic or cultural. Their function can be to change something in society, like a political association, or to express themselves in a way that meets the members' social needs, like a choral society or a bridge club. Statistics show that 79 percent of Denmark's business leaders have been active in associations before the age of 30. Respectively, 94 percent, 92 percent and 88 percent of managers with experience in associations believe that these years of involvement benefited their social skills and interpersonal skills and gave them a strong network. Ninety-nine percent of Denmark's governors believe it promotes young people's professional skills to be active in voluntary associations.

Being in a social group like this is a very big part of being Danish. They like finding ways to work together and support each other in these social groups and this is also true with how they work as a family.

"We are also a team in our family," Iben says. "It isn't expressed like this but it is something we foster. The kitchen isn't only my domain, for example. My girls know that they can come and help peel carrots or set the table. Together we make it run. And together we create hygge."

In fact, Danes are known for being easy to work with and likeable worldwide. This is because they are excellent team players. They help others to help themselves and they are humble even when they are stars. And who doesn't appreciate a humble star?

Singing and hygge

An interesting place Danes like to create hygge is in their affection for singing. From Christmas lunches to birthdays to baptisms and weddings, if there is a song-worthy event, they will most likely be singing.

The songs they sing are often specially written for an occasion to be handed out and sung to a popular tune. These homemade lyrics are frequently hilarious and everyone joins in discovering the words while singing together. Otherwise, the songs they sing come from a national songbook called "Højskolesangbogen". The national songbook contains over 572 songs and hymns, which are divided into several sections so you can find the occasion you are looking for more easily. It has sold over 2.8 million copies (and there are 5.5 million people in Denmark) since the first edition was issued in 1894. The Danish singing tradition dates back to the feasts of the nobility and aristocracy in the late Middle Ages, but over time it has been cultivated and is now more common than ever.

Nick Stewart from Oxford Brooke University has conducted research on choir singers and has found that not only does singing in a troop make people happier but it also makes them feel that they are part of a meaningful group. The synchronicity of moving and breathing while singing together creates a strong feeling of connectedness. Moreover, studies have found that groups of singers have actually been able to synchronize their heartbeats while singing. Singing together releases the "happy" hormone oxytocin, which lowers stress and increases feelings of trust and bonding. One only has to try group singing, once you stop feeling silly, to feel these powerful effects.

Social ties and stress levels

The happiness level of the Danes isn't the only proof of the effectiveness of togetherness and "hyggelige" ties. Lots of research back this up.

Researchers at Brigham Young University and the University of North Carolina at Chapel Hill pooled data from 148 studies on health outcomes and its correlation to social relationships. They gathered every research paper on the topic they could find, involving more than 300,000 men and women across the developed world. They found that people with poor social connections had on average 50 percent higher odds of dying earlier (about 7.5 years earlier) than people with robust social ties. That difference in longevity is about as large as the mortality difference between smokers and non-smokers. And it is larger than any health risks associated with many other well-known lifestyle factors such as lack of exercise and obesity.

In another famous experiment on health and social ties, Sheldon College at Carnegie Mellon University exposed hundreds of healthy volunteers to the common cold virus and then quarantined them for several days. The results showed that the quarantined participants with more social connections were less likely to develop a cold than the participants who were more isolated in their lives.

The immune system of people with lots of friends simply worked better. They were better able to fight off the cold virus, often without any symptoms. Seeing as stress hormones seem to have an effect on the immune response, it makes sense that a strong social life helps the immune system stay strong by keeping physiological stress in check.

A research group in Chicago studied this effect and confirmed it. Social support does, in fact, help manage stress. If we know we have people we can talk to or turn to for help in difficult times, we are more ready to face life's challenges without breaking down. We are more resilient. Being vulnerable with someone is a huge distribution of the stress we carry to get it off our backs. Many people try to be tough and stoic and keep things inside. This goes back to this idea of individualism and being able to do it on your own. Some are afraid of being judged or seeming weak. Some people don't want to bother others with their problems and so they shut down. But this not only lowers the immune system response, it also makes you unhappier. Research shows that people who try to be tough in a tragedy will suffer for a much longer period than those who share their emotions and are vulnerable with others. Something to think about the next time you are going through a difficult period.

New moms and the Danish Way of togetherness

This trend can particularly be seen in new mothers. New mothers are under an incredible amount of stress struggling with their new role. Lack of sleep and all the tasks in front of new parents can be overwhelming and incredibly difficult to cope with. Yet, research shows that the reaction new mothers often have to this difficult period is to reduce the amount of social support rather than increase it. This is paradoxical because it is exactly what they shouldn't do. Support from friends, family members and parent groups has been clearly proven to help new mothers deal better with stress and thereby help them see their children in a more positive light. This improves everyone's quality of life, particularly the growing child. The more parents surround themselves with social support, the healthier and happier the baby will grow up to be.

In Denmark, when a woman gives birth a local midwife gets her details and contacts her within the first week to check in and see if she and the baby are ok. But it is not only to make sure they are ok, it is also to give her the names and contact details of all the other women in her close neighborhood or surrounding areas who have just had a baby too. This is even related to if it is the first baby or second or third so the women are well matched up. These women form groups and go to them once a week to share with each other and provide support. The other mothers in the group also act as a sponsor and will check in on a mother if she doesn't come. They will call her or go to her house to make sure she is ok and has contact with others she can share with. These groups are a fundamental support during a very difficult time and a very natural part of being a new mother in Denmark. One should not underestimate the importance of telling their story again and again. It has a clarifying and therapeutic effect.

The Danish Way of hygge
We have talked a lot about social support, togetherness and the importance of hygge. But let me give a personal example of the day I understood what it really was.

It was a sunny, fresh day. I was lying in the hammock in my sister-in-law's backyard under a large plum tree with my husband and young son and daughter squeezed in between us. We were wrapped up like a swinging burrito. Some with eyes opened, some with eyes shut. I pushed with one foot hanging lazily out of the hammock to keep us swaying back and forth. The wind was rustling the trees loudly; flickering rays of sun shone through the leaves in kaleidoscope patterns on our faces. It was a combination of touch, the sounds of warm nature and the smell of my baby son's downy hair. I could feel his heartbeat, the warmth of my husband's leg next to mine. I was holding my daughter's foot, who was cuddled up quietly with him. We were all there.

"Ah, I see you are enjoying some family hygge over here," his sister said as she came to invite us in for lunch. And that, I thought, after 13 years together was hygge in a nutshell.

It's a feeling as well as a way of being. It is eliminating the confusion and hysteria of all else. It is choosing to enjoy the most important, meaningful moments of our lives—those with our children and family and friends and respecting them as important. It is keeping them simple, making the atmosphere nice and leaving our troubles behind. It is wanting to be there in those moments, choosing to be there and helping contribute to having a cozy time. With a big family, this takes effort because like all team projects, it is working together for a shared goal. This is opposite from being an individual and shining out. Everyone has to want it and respect it. You can't work alone on a team and win the objective. Everyone plays a part. If we are all willing to contribute to creating a cozy time together, it dramatically improves family get-togethers, which dramatically affects our well-being and happiness.

How can we practice the Danish Way of togetherness and hygge?

1. TAKE THE HYGGE OATH

Make a pact with the whole family at the next gathering to not think about "I" but about being in the moment and trying to help and make things run without conflict and controversy. Print out the "hygge oath" to learn more at thedanishway.com.

2. BE IN THE MOMENT TOGETHER

Everyone should agree to leave their daily stressors at the door. Don't focus on the bad things in your or someone else's life: try not to talk negatively about someone too much. Everyone must make an effort to be in that moment together. Keep it lively and jovial and non-accusatory. Kids mirror this behavior and that can only be a good thing.

3. PRACTICE PREFRAMING

Prepare yourself for a get-together so you get the most out of it without putting on your usual prescription glasses to the world or your family. Remember that stress-free get-togethers with your family greatly increase well-being. We are often stuck in our ways with different family members. Change it. Use empathy, reframing and preframing to help.

4. HAVE FUN TOGETHER

Play games inside and out that everyone can take part in.
Kids love this. Stop thinking about your own wants for those
gatherings and get out there and have fun.

5. MAKE IT COZY

Make the atmosphere cozy (light candles at night) and have nice
food and drinks.

6. STOP COMPLAINING

Stop complaining and see where you can help out. This alone, if
everyone agrees to do it, makes a huge difference.

7. PRACTICE REFRAMING IF YOU GET STRESSED

It is such a powerful tool. Everything can be reframed. Remember,
by doing this you pass this on to your kids, making them better at
dealing with their own stressful reactions.

8. Keep things simple to appreciate hygge

We often have so many toys (both for adults and kids, like TV) that drown out the simple things like the sound of the wind in the trees and the funny, amusing things our kids do. Distractions take away from hygge, which is about appreciating the most basic and real things. Keep it simple.

9. Make the kids keep it simple

Use fewer toys and TVs, iPhones and iPads. These should be avoided in gatherings so the kids, too, can be more present together. Play games.

10. Be connected

Try to learn and practice having a cozy time together. Learning to hygge together, your kids will pass this on and this makes for better family connectedness overall.

11. Encourage play

Invite the older children to play with the younger ones in "play", not play on an electrical device. Leave them paints or let them play outside but have rules for the gatherings that they are technology free (or limit it to certain times).

12. TEAM BUILDING

Organize more team-building activities for children to encourage working together. Implement the values from the other chapters. Make scavenger hunts, build something, organize a tournament. Be creative.

13. CONFIDE AND SHARE

When you are down or in a difficult moment, confide and share with your good friends and loved ones you trust. Remember, this reduces stress and helps you get over it faster.

14. START A MOTHERS' GROUP

Find out who is in your neighborhood or close by and build a support network. Try focusing on the values of the Danish Way. This support has been proven to be extremely beneficial since the mothers see their children in a better light.

15. PRACTICE EMPATHY

Be vulnerable. Be compassionate. Be empathic. This will help all of your social ties and interactions. Practicing empathy will be the single biggest factor in helping you reframe. It is much easier to reframe when we try to really see things from someone else's perspective.

16. TEACH YOUR CHILDREN THAT THE FAMILY IS A TEAM

Teach your children how they can see the family as a team and what part they can play. Show them how they can help and contribute. This will help them grow up to have better social ties, which contributes to well-being. Hygge can be trained and learned and makes for happier people overall.

17. HYGGE IS NOT ABOUT SIZE

Remember that "hygge" can be done with one or two people. It isn't only limited to big family gatherings. You can declare a "hygge night", for instance, during the week where you implement the rules above.

18. SING

Sound silly? It works! It's fun and it's very hyggeligt! Kids absolutely love this and adults do too.

o o o o

Where Do We Go from Here?

And so the question arises again. After 40 years of being voted the happiest people in the world, what is it that has kept the Danes at the top of the happiness charts for so long? As we have seen in *The Danish Way*, it is, quite simply the way they raise their children. It is a chain that continues on and on and repeats itself through the generations.

The Danish Way of Parenting is a guide to help parents utilize this tried-and-tested philosophy here at home. It has worked in Denmark for centuries in creating self-assured, confident, strongly centered, happy and resilient adults, and it can work for us.

As a parent, it is important that we first examine ourselves to be able to really see what we like and don't like about our reactions. By identifying what our default settings are, our natural inclinations as parents, we are better able to see where that change is needed. Taking the time to see ourselves in the mirror, and see what we are repeating from our own family cycles, is the first step towards powerful change and powerful parenting.

Once we have identified our default settings in the acronym parent— p-play, a-authenticity, r-reframing, e-empathy, n-no ultimatums, t-togetherness—*The Danish Way* lays out the main lines of thinking in order to help us have better output as a parent.

Play tells us that by allowing our children more time to engage in unstructured play, we are giving them a gift of developing many life skills. Resilience, coping skills, negotiation and self-control are just a few of the valuable lessons learned in play. By allowing them more time to play, we are helping them develop crucial stress management skills as a child, which lowers their likelihood of anxiety as an adult. Play helps develop an internal locus of control and fosters happiness.

Authenticity tells us that by being honest with ourselves and our children, we are creating a much stronger internal compass in our kids because they learn to trust their emotions. Teaching honesty to ourselves and to our children is a strong character value. And remember that all emotions are ok. We also learned that the praise we give our children is monumental in how they come to see themselves in the world. Giving empty praise or focusing too much on being smart can set kids up for being insecure. By engaging in process praise, we foster a growth mindset rather than a fixed mindset, which contributes to a more persistent, deeply confident and resilient individual.

In Reframing, we talked about the power to change our own and our children's perceptions about life. How we choose to see things affects the way we feel things. Realistic optimists don't ignore negative information, they just focus on the other information at hand to write a richer, more loving story about themselves, their children and life in general. Reframing is so powerful because it can literally change our experience of the world and it makes our own and our children's lives happier in the process. Passing on the skill of reframing to our children may be one of the greatest gifts we can give. It ensures happier adults because they learn to frame their story that way. And then this skill gets repeated and becomes a default setting.

In Empathy, we looked at how the level of empathy has dropped in our society and the level of narcissism has increased. Part of this is because of the American way of individualism. However, research shows that we are far more wired for empathy than for selfishness than previously thought. By being less judgmental and shaming, we can better understand the vulnerability in ourselves and in others, which brings us closer together. Being closer to others, forging deeper, more forgiving relationships makes us happier overall. Practicing empathy teaches children to respect others and themselves and this makes for a more profound sense of well-being.

In No Ultimatums, we saw how power struggles can lead us to lose our temper. Many people scream or use physical punishment as a form of discipline. We lose our control and yet we expect our children not to. In an authoritarian parenting style parents lose the trust and closeness with their kids, which is replaced with fear. It works in the short term but can have consequences in the long run. The Danish, more diplomatic parenting style fosters trust and resilience in children. Children who feel respected and understood, and in turn who are helped to understand and respect rules, develop a much stronger internal locus of control and ultimately grow up to be happier, more emotionally stable adults.

Finally, in Togetherness and Hygge, we learned how close relationships are one of the biggest predictors of a person's happiness level. By learning how to "hygge" or cozy around, we can improve our family get-togethers to make them more pleasant and memorable experiences for our kids. By leaving the "I" at the door and focusing on the "we", we can eliminate a lot of the unnecessary drama and negativity sometimes associated with family get-togethers. Happy families and strong social support yield happier kids.

As we said earlier, you may already be familiar with some of the concepts in *The Danish Way* or you may have been completely unfamiliar with them. You may already practice some of the Danish methods or you may practice none of them. We are convinced that if you take away even a few of the methods from this book and incorporate them into your life, you will be on the right track to raising happier kids.

If you want to find out more about the Danish Way, please go to thedanishway.com website. There you will find tips, book suggestions and information on P-A-R-E-N-T.

We think that together, parents and teachers can support each other in promoting the Danish Way to raise happier, more resilient kids. We all need support. By building a community together with the goal of practicing some of these tenets, we can cultivate some of the happiest people in the world in our own backyards. If you believe in what the results say year after year, then please get on board and let's make it happen!

NOTES

For those who want more information or facts about our sources and references, you can find inspiration here.

What's the Secret to Their Happiness?

OECD (Organisation for Economic Co-operation and Development) study. OECD better life index measures the well-being of different countries. www.OECD.org

The first World Happiness Report (http://www.earth.columbia.edu/articles/view/2960), commissioned for the UN Conference on Happiness, held in April 2012, drew international attention as a landmark first survey of the state of global happiness. The World Happiness Report 2013 (http://unsdsn.org/resources/publications/world-happiness-report-2013/) found Denmark to have the happiest people. This is not the first time the Danes have been awarded this prestigious title. Back in 1973, the European Commission set up a "Eurobarometer" to find out about its citizens. Since then, member states have been surveyed about well-being and happiness. Denmark has topped the table every year since 1973!

60 Minutes program. http://www.cbsnews.com/news/and-the-happiest-place-on-earth-is/

Oprah. http://www.oprah.com/world/Inside-the-Lives-of-Women-Around-the-World

Cultural Differences and Paradigm Shifts

Harkness, Sarah (2005): *Parental ethnotheories*, Super.

Themes and variations: Parental ethnotheories in Western cultures. In K. Rubin & O.B. Chung (Eds.), Parental beliefs, parenting, and child development in cross-cultural perspective. London: Psychology Press.

Antidepressant use went up 400 percent from 2005-2008. National Center for Health statistics. http://www.cdc.gov/nchs/data/databriefs/db76.htm

Attention deficit has become the go-to diagnosis, increasing by an average of 5.5 percent a year between 2003 and 2007. http://www.cdc.gov/ncbddd/adhd/data.html/

5.2 million children between the ages of 3 and 17 had been given diagnoses of attention deficit hyperactivity disorder. http://www.cdc.gov/nchs/fastats/adhd.htm

Default Settings and Why They Need to Be Examined

As a mom and dad—being aware of yourself and choosing your behavior is the first step towards powerful life change.
http://www.boernogunge.dk/internet/boernogunge.nsf/0/7F933F515B65A7B3C1256C64002D2029?opendocument

Play

"Remarkably, over the last 50 years, opportunities for children to play freely have declined continuously and dramatically in the United States and other developed nations, and that decline continues with serious negative consequences for children's physical, mental and social development," said Guest Editor Peter Gray, a research professor of psychology at Boston College. http://www.bc.edu/offices/pubaf/news/2011_jun-aug/petergray_freeplay08252011.html

Resilience and success: *True Grit. Scientific American Mind*. August 2013.

The first actual pedagogy based on an educational theory in 1871 by husband and wife Erna and Niels Juel Hansen who were inspired by Friedrich Fröbel (1782-1852) and made the first Fröbel kindergarten. For the first time, play becomes important in Denmark. Fröbel understood that children's play comes from themselves. Play is a natural expression of specific needs, and therefore, he highlighted play as a pedagogical method to promote children's development. Since then, there has been a strong flow of free play in Denmark. http://www.bupl.dk/iwfile/BALG-8RQDV8/$file/EnPaedagogiskHistorie.pdf

Internal vs. external locus of control. http://en.wikipedia.org/wiki/Locus_of_control

Children, adults and adolescents who exhibit the helpless feelings associated with an external locus of control are predisposed to anxiety and depression. Ho Cheung William Li and Oi Kwan Joyce Chung, *The Relationship Between Children's Locus of Control and Their Anticipatory Anxiety*, Public Health Nursing 26 (2009): 153–60.

Study over a 50-year period shows a rise in external locus of control in children from 1960-2002. Jean M. Twenge, Liqing Zhang and Charles Im, *It's Beyond My Control: A Cross-Temporal Meta-Analysis of Increasing Externality in Locus of Control, 1960–2002*, Personality and Social Psychology Review 8 (2004): 308–19.

The Russian psychologist Lev Vygotsky (1896-1934) was interested in development in early childhood and how people extend their existing knowledge. He created, in his short life, a theory of learning that was strangely visionary. His thinking has to this day had a major influence on the scope and teaching in Danish schools. It is therefore highly relevant to familiarize oneself with Vygotsky's thinking, and how it is translated in a Danish context. He is particularly known for the concept of which he called "the zone of proximal development". It is a zone covering the area of the child's independence, and that it is possible for the child to know and be able to cooperate within that zone. Strandberg, Leif (2009): *Vygotskij i praksis*. Akademisk Forlag.

Michael White, founder of the field of narrative therapy (1948-2008), was inspired by Lev Vygotsky's thoughts of the zone of proximal development. He developed maps for scaffolding talks, which are built over five questions or inquiry categories and they support gradual and progressive movement through the zone of proximal learning. White writes about Vygotsky: "By studying social cooperation, he observed that adult carers structure children's learning in ways that allow them to move from the familiar and the routine performance of what is possible for them to know and achieve. He described the phenomenon as a movement through a learning zone, which he called 'the zone of proximal development'. This zone marks the area where children are able to learn and achieve something on their own, and that it is possible for the child to learn and achieve, in cooperation with others."
White, Michael (2008): *Kort Over Narrative Landskaber* (s. 274). Hans Reitzels Forlag. (Maps of Narrative Practice)

Pushing kids to read earlier isn't better. Renowned professor and developmental psychologist Dr. David Elkind, author of such bestsellers as *The Hurried Child*, reminds us that "there is no correlation between pushing children into early reading and later academic success." What's even more disconcerting is that children who have attended academic, rather than developmental, preschools tend to exhibit higher levels of anxiety and self-esteem issues, along with reading scores that, in the long term, are no better. Pressure and anxiety are not necessary components of a solid education for your youngster and, in fact, can have long-term negative effects. http://www.heyquitpushing.com/why-sooner-inst-better.html

Studies on rhesus monkeys and domestic rats deprived of playmates show excessive fear or inappropriate aggression. For reviews of such play-deprivation research, see Peter LaFreniere: *Evolutionary Functions of Social Play: Life Histories, Sex Differences, and Emotion Regulation*. American Journal of Play 3 (2011): 464–88; and Pellis et al.: *The Function of Play in the Development of the Social Brain,* 278–96.

Animals allowed a playmate for even an hour a day developed more normally. Pellis S. M., Pellis, V. C. (2011): *Rough and tumble play: Training and using the social brain*. In A. D. Pellgrini (Ed.): *The Oxford handbook of the development of play* (pp. 245-259). Oxford, UK: Oxford University Press. Also: Bell, H. C., Pellis, S. M. & Kolb, B. *Juvenile peer play experience and the development of the orbitofrontal and medial prefrontal cortex*, Behavioral and Brain Research (2010): 207, 7-13.

Exposing the brains of baby animals to stress changes them in ways that make them less responsive to stress. Engaging in play that excites fight or flight instincts is learning how to master stress. [3] Pellis, S. M., Pellis, V. C. (2011): *Rough and tumble play: Training and using the social brain.* In A. D. Pellgrini (Ed.), *The Oxford handbook of the development of play* (pp. 245-259). Oxford, UK: Oxford University Press. Sergio M. Pellis, Vivien C. Pellis, and Heather C. Bell (2010): *The Function of Play in the Development of the Social Brain*, American Journal of Play 2, 278–96.

Individuals suffering anxiety disorders describe losing emotional control as one of their greatest fears. David H. Barlow (2002): *Anxiety and Its Disorders: The Nature and Treatment of Anxiety and Panic*, 2nd ed.

Level of playfulness in preschoolers directly correlated with coping. *The relationship between playfulness and coping skills in preschoolers: a pilot study*. Saunders, Sayer M., Goodale A. http://www.ncbi.nlm.nih.gov/pubmed/10200846

Adolescent boys with a higher level of playfulness had better coping skills. *The association between playfulness and coping in adolescents*. Hess LM, Bundy AC. Phys Occup Ther Pediatr. 2003; 23(2):5-17.

Research shows juvenile animals play to deal with the unexpected. Marek Spinka, Ruth C. Newberry and Marc Bekoff: *Mammalian Play: Training for the Unexpected*, Quarterly Review of Biology 76 (2001): 141–68.

Children learn to deal with conflict, control and cooperation to keep playing. LaFreniere: *Evolutionary Functions of Social Play*, American Journal of Play 3 (2011): 464–88.

Children interaction in play—they negotiate roles and rules.
Broström, Stig (2002): *Børns Lærerige Leg*, Psyke & Logos, 23, 451-469.
Stig Broström is a trained educator, Cand.pæd.pæd. and PhD in early childhood education. He is an associate professor at the Danish University of Education.

Play Patrol exists because of collaborations between "Dansk Skoleidræt and Danish schools". Danish School Sport is a national sports organization that has as its main objective to promote learning, health and well-being through sports, play and exercise for all students in the school. "By offering activities in the school's various arenas—i.e., immediately before and after school, in the classroom and during recess—we will, in cooperation with its schools, give students the opportunity to experience the joy of sports and physical activities. We do this based on the belief that positive experiences associated with physical activity build the foundation for good habits. And that's what makes the students more able to make healthy choices in life, today and in their future." www.legepatruljen.dk

The practice of self-control. *Lev Vygotsky: The Role of Play in Development, in Mind in Society*: The Development of Higher Psychological Processes, ed. Michael Cole, Vera John-Steiner, Sylvia Scribner, and Ellen Souberman (1978): 92–104.

Lego was dubbed "The toy of the century" by *Fortune* magazine.
Originally made in wood and then plastic.
www.visitdenmark.dk/da/danmark/design/lego-et-dansk-verdensbrand

Learning by playing is the best way to fill young children with knowledge, say two Danish researchers. There is clear scientific evidence that children learn best through play. Pernille Hviid, professor of psychology and Bo Stjerne Thomsen, PhD in architecture and media technology and director of Research and Learning in The Lego Foundation. *Children can play their way to more learning in school*; June 23, 2014.
http://sciencenordic.com/children-can-play-their-way-more-learning-school

Kompan playground. www.kompan.dk

Sensory-rich environments coupled with play promote cortical growth. *Learning and Changes in the Brain* by Silvia Helena Cardoso, PhD and Renato M.E. Sabbatini, PhD
http://lecerveau.mcgill.ca/flash/capsules/articles_pdf/changes_brain.pdf

Pediatricians in the US release guidelines that say play is healthy: "Unstructured play time is more valuable for the developing brain than electronic media. Children learn to think creatively, problem solve, and develop reasoning and motor skills at early ages through unstructured, unplugged play. Free play also teaches them how to entertain themselves." http://www.aap.org/en-us/about-the-aap/aap-press-room/Pages/Babies-and-Toddlers-Should-Learn-from-Play-Not-Screens.aspx

Extra Resources and Further Inspiration

Associate Professor at the School of Education Hans Henrik Knoop, University of Aarhus, head of research of positive psychology.
Psychology and brain research tell us today much about how education can be an exciting, professionally efficient and creative experience. He describes how to combine respect for "the well-being and learning" and respect for "the wishes and requirements" with learning and creativity, which can be an exhilarating, effective and creative experience. Knoop, Hans Henrik (2002): *Play, learning and creativity—why happy children learn more*. Aschehoug.

Educators can work with play and learning—how play can be instructive and how targeted learning activities can be in the nature of play. Johansson, Eva & Ingrid Samuelsson (2011): *Lærerig leg—børns læring gennem samspil*. Dafolo.

Research mapping and research assessment of Scandinavian research in the year 2009 in institutions for 0- to 6-year-olds (preschool). Play and learning in everyday life. http://www.eva.dk/dagtilbud/bakspejlet/forskningskortlaegning-2009. Clearinghouse—Forskningsserien, 2011. Number 07.

Bo Stjerne Thomsen, director of Research and Learning in The LEGO Foundation, agrees that schools should use games more in education. He says: "Children learn through play. They are curious and explore things. So they create things and share with others. There is clear scientific evidence that children learn best through play."

Associate professor of psychology Pernille Hviid emphasizes that "learning through play is not the priority of the basic skills that Danish and mathematics teachers teach students today. This is not a rejection of conventional wisdom, but a chance to let it interact with the imagination. If it becomes a reality, the next generation could not just take over society, it will also be geared to develop it for the future."
http://videnskab.dk/miljo-naturvidenskab/born-skal-lege-sig-klogere-i-skolen

Freeman, Jennifer, David Epston and Dean Lobovits (1997): *Playful approaches to serious problems*, W. W. Norton & Company.

Authenticity

Sad movies make you happy. S. Knobloch-Westerwick, Y. Gong, H. Hagner, L. Kerbeykian. *Tragedy Viewers Count Their Blessings: Feeling Low on Fiction Leads to Feeling High on Life*. Communication Research: (2012).

Oliver, M. B. & Raney, A. A. *Entertainment as pleasurable and meaningful: Differentiating hedonic and eudaimonic motivations for entertainment consumption.* Journal of Communication (2011): 64, 984-1004. http://blogs.scientificamerican.com/guestblog/2013/09/29/tv-so-good-it-hurts-the-psychology-of-watching-breaking-bad/
Debate over the ending of The Little Mermaid. Some scholars consider the ending with a happy ending to be an unnatural addition. http://en.wikipedia.org/wiki/The_Little_Mermaid

The Wallet Test, Reader's Digest (1995): pp 17-19.

To understand the feelings, thoughts and intentions that underline the child's actions. Hagelquist, Janne Østergaard & Marianne Køhler Skov (2014): *Mentalisering i pædagogik og terapi*, Hans Reitzels Forlag.

Humility is not ignorance of who or what you are, but rather the acceptance and recognition of what is not in relationship to the other.
www.etik.dk/klummen-etisk-set/ydmyghed-er-en-sand-dyd

Dweck, C. S. (2006): *Mindset: The New Psychology of Success.* New York, Random House.

Dweck C.S. (1999): *Self-Theories: Their role in motivation, personality and development.* Philadelphia, Taylor and Francis/Psychology Press.

Blackwell, L., Trzesniewski, K. & Dweck, C. S. *Implicit theories of intelligence predict achievement across an adolescent transition: A longitudinal study and an intervention.* Child Development (2007): 78, 246–263.

Studies on 5th graders looks at praise for intelligence and how it creates a fixed mindset. Mueller, C. M. & Dweck, C. S. *Intelligence praise can undermine motivation and performance.* Journal of Personality and Social Psychology (1998): 75, 33–52.

Brain's plasticity. Doidge, N. (2007): *The brain that changes itself: Stories of personal triumph from the frontiers of brain science*. New York: Viking.

Persistance and dedication when faced with obstacles that count Ericsson, K. A., Charness, N., Feltovich, P. J. & Hoffman, R. R. (Eds.). (2006): *The Cambridge handbook of expertise and expert performance*. New York: Cambridge University Press. http://www.nytimes.com/2008/07/06/business/06unbox.html?_r=0

Extra Resources and Further Inspiration

Happiness: love people, not pleasure. http://www.nytimes.com/2014/07/20/opinion/sunday/arthur-c-brooks-love-people-not-pleasure.html?_r=1

The resistance can be strengthened. www.psykiatrifonden.dk

Reframing

Realistic optimism. Resilience and success. *True Grit. Scientific American Mind*. August 2013.

"More than education, more than experience, more than training, a person's level of resilience will determine who succeeds and who fails. That's true in the cancer ward, it's true in the Olympics, and it's true in the boardroom."
Dean M. Becker. *How Resilience Works*, Harvard Business Review, May 2002.

Numerous studies show that when we deliberately reinterpret an event to feel better about it, it decreases activity in areas of the brain involved in the processing of negative emotions such as the amygdala and the insula and increases activity in areas of the brain involved in cognitive control and adaptive integrations. Oschner Beck, A.T. & Emery, G. (1985): *Anxiety disorders and phobias: A cognitive perspective*.

New York, Basic Books. Borkovec, T.D. & Whisman, M.A. (in press): *Psychosocial treatment for generalized anxiety disorder*. In M. Mavissakalian & R. Prien (Eds.), *Anxiety disorders: Psychological and pharmacological treatments*. Washington, DC: American Psychiatric Press.

Angry faces. Sheppes, G., Scheibe, S., Suri, G., Radu, P., Blechert, J. & Gross, J. J. *Emotion regulation choice: A conceptual framework and supporting evidence*. Journal of Experimental Psychology—General (2014): 143(1), 163-181.

Spiders and snakes. Shurick, A. A., Hamilton, J. R., Harris, L. T., Roy, A. K., Gross, J. J., Phelps, E. A. (2012). *Durable effects of cognitive restructuring on conditioned fear.* Emotion. Advance online publication. doi: 10.1037/a0029143.

We can often get to express ourselves in a conversation with ourselves, families and colleagues in a negatively defining way: "I'm depressed," "She is impossible" and "He never listens." Rasmussen, Svend Aage (2003): *Det fjendtlige sprog—Refleksioner over udviklinger i psykiatrien* s. 229-245, Universitetsforlaget, Fokus.

Reframing should be in the water we drink. https://www.udemy.com/the-neuroscience-of-reframing-and-how-to-do-it/

"It is through the personal narrative, we take the lessons learned from the events in our life to us and give them meaning. It is through the personal narrative, we link our life events to sequences that unfold over time according to specific themes."
(p. 143) White, Michael (2006): *Narrativ teori*. Hans Reitzels Forlag. (The Narrative Perspective in Therapy)

Man is interpretive by nature, and we try to make events meaningful. A narrative is like a thread that weaves events together and forms a story. Such stories are very much to shape our lives. By putting events together in an alternate history, it can open up new ways of seeing themselves and the world. Morgan, Alice (2005): *Narrative Samtaler*. Hans Reitzels Forlag. (What is narrative therapy?)

To facilitate this process, which White calls "reauthoring", the adult can ask curious questions of the child about what he calls "action landscape" and "awareness of the landscape." In therapeutic conversations, these concepts allow the therapist to create a context where people are able to ascribe meaning to many of the overlooked but important events in their lives. White, Michael (2008): *Kort over narrative landskaber*. Hans Reitzels Forlag. (Maps of Narrative Practice)

A problem is only a problem if it is referred to as a problem. Holmgren, Allan (2014): Personal conversation, but also from: Holmgren, Anette + et.al (2010): *Fra Terapi til Praksis — en brugsbog i narrativ praksis*. Hans Reitzels Forlag.

We want to understand meaning in action.
Bruner, Jerome (1999): *Mening i handling*, Forlaget Klim. (Acts of Meaning)

Unique outcome or also called "exception" may also be classified as initiatives. Unique outcome is always present in people's lives, but usually missed and lost. White, Michael (2008): *Kort over narrative landskaber*. Hans Reitzels Forlag. (Maps of Narrative Practice)

To separate actions from the person is also called externalization. Externalizing helps to dissolve or deconstruct the problem and the ability to create stories around it resourcefully. White, Michael (2006): *Narrativ teori*. Hans Reitzels Forlag. (The Narrative Perspective in Therapy)

Talking about problems so that they become separated from the person is a linguistic practice that gives space to alternative descriptions of children so they can express themselves in a way that their favorite stories are more accessible. (p. 76)
White, Michael & Morgan, Alice (2007): *Narrativ terapi med børn og deres familier*; Akademisk Forlag. (Narrative Therapy with Children and Their Families)

"I have emphasized and illustrated the potential of externalizing conversations to (a) assist people to break from negative identity conclusions, and to (b) pave the way for the introduction of other conversations which contribute to the exploration of and generation of more positive identity conclusions. These positive identity conclusions are not stand-alone phenomena. They are associated with specific knowledges of life and practices of living." White, Michael: *Narrative Practice and the Unpacking of Identity Conclusions. www.psybc.com/pdfs/library/WHITE.pdf*

"You can and must always tell a different story than the dominant story. Each story gives no depth, no perspective in the recital and in the description. (p. 11) We find it more relevant to thicken these tales than to lavish our children with superficial praise." White, Michael (2006): *Narrativ teori*. Hans Reitzels Forlag. (The Narrative Perspective in Therapy)

Empathy

Level of empathy has dropped 50 percent. *Changes in Dispositional Empathy in American College Students over Time: A Meta-Analysis*. S. Konrath, E. O'Brien and C. Hsing in Personality and Social Psychology Review. Published online August 5, 2010.

Narcissism has risen significantly and linearly. Jean M. Twenge and Joshua D. Foster, "Birth Cohort Increases in Narcissistic Personality Traits Among American College Students, 1982–2009," *Social Psychological and Personality Science* 1 (2010): 99–106; Jean M. Twenge, "Egos Inflating Over Time: A Cross-Temporal Meta-Analysis of the Narcissistic Personality Inventory," *Journal of Personality* 76 (2008): 875–901.
Peter Gray writes about why he suspects narcissism is increasing in America. http://www.psychologytoday.com/blog/freedom-learn/201401/why-is-narcissism-increasing-among-young-americans

Narcissism has reached new heights. *The Narcissism Epidemic*: *Living in the Age of Entitlement*. J. M. Twenge and W. K. Campbell. Free Press, 2009.

For many years in America, we have believed that humans, like nature, are fundamentally selfish, aggressive and competitive.http://healthland.time.com/2012/10/08/is-human-nature-fundamentally-selfish-or-altruistic/

Brene Brown. "People are afraid to be vulnerable for disconnecting". https://www.ted.com/talks/brene_brown_on_vulnerability

"We are the most in debt, obese, addicted and medicated society in the world." https://www.ted.com/talks/brene_brown_on_vulnerability

Social brain. Lieberman M. D. (2013): *Social: Why our brains are wired to connect.* New York, Crown.

Lieberman believes that we are not only wired for self-interest but also in the welfare of others. https://www.youtube.com/watch?v=NNhk3owF7RQ&feature=kp

Prisoner's Dilemma. http://www.nytimes.com/2013/11/03/books/review/social-by-matthew-d-lieberman.html?_r=1.

Empathy studies on animals. From an evolution standpoint, empathy was a valuable impulse that helped us survive in groups. *The Age of Empathy: Nature's Lessons for a Kinder Society.* Frans de Waal. Harmony Books.

"An Interview with Frans de Waal." American Scientist. http://www.americanscientist.org/bookshelf/pub/an-interview-with-frans-de-waal

http://www.ted.com/talks/frans_de_waal_do_animals_have_morals

Only when scientists began studying infants in interaction with their mothers did the picture change crucially. When the evidence became clear that children are born with the ability to do what Professor Daniel N. Stern calls "fading"—i.e., the ability to tune into the mother's emotions and moods, and later on with other people. This brings us back to the basics of the human capacity for empathy—the ability to empathize, to sense and understand the other's feelings.

http://www.family-lab.com/about/jesper-juul-articles/item/empati-3

The midbrain or mesencephalon contains portions of "the limbic system", which you might say is the brain's chemical factory. The limbic system is very important for our social behavior and emotions. "Between brain" consists of thalamus, hypothalamus and pituitary gland.

www.tekno.dk/undervisning/materiale/artikel2.pdf

Daniel Siegel, http://cultureofempathy.com/References/Experts/Daniel-Siegel.htm

"Empathy is not a luxury, it is a necessity". Daniel Siegel and Edwin Rutsch: *Dialogues on how to build a culture of empathy*. http://www.youtube.com/watch?v=XIzTdXdhU0w

The very first experience of empathy: When parents react to the child's different expressions. That way you communicate to your child that you are there and want to help. www.voresborn.dk/barn-3-8/psykologi-og-udvikling/4254-laer-dit-barn-at-vaere-god-mod-andre

"Very young babies react to how other people feel. Studies show that infants respond to the crying from others by being scared or anxious, and some even start to cry." Charlotte Clemmensen is a trained psychologist from the Danish University of Education (Danmarks Pædagogiske Universitet). www.voresborn.dk/barn-3-8/psykologi-og-udvikling/4254-laer-dit-barn-at-vaere-god-mod-andre

Eighteen-month-old toddlers show that they will almost always try to help an adult who is visibly struggling with a task. http://www.eva.mpg.de/psycho/videos/children_cabinet.mpg

If the adult is reaching for something, the toddler will try to hand it to him, or if they see an adult drop something accidentally, they will pick it up. On the other hand, if the same adult throws something to the ground forcefully, they won't pick it up for him. Warneken, F. & Tomasello, M. *Altruistic helping in human infants and young chimpanzees.* Science (2006): 311, 1301-1303. http://www.theguardian.com/science/2013/oct/12/babies-moral-life

Children learn first and foremost from their parents and by using empathy and compassion, these parents pass it on to their children.
www.family-lab.com/about/jesper-juul-articles/item/empati-3

The young child learns through imitation of what is happening in the environment, and through dialogue, linking words and objects/ideas together. In the company of other kids, children are educated on the ability to read and communicate. It often occurs through imitation, body language, facial expressions and humorous incident.
http://dcum.dk/boernemiljoe/sprog

Types of families that can affect children's ability to empathize. Jesper Juul is an internationally renowned public speaker, author, family therapist and educator with activities in more than 15 countries around the globe. His findings have since been confirmed by both neuroscience and relational psychology and constitute the basis for a new paradigm and perspective in the study of and principles for dealing with families as well as the interaction between children, youth and adults.
Juul, Jesper (2008): *Din kompetente familie*. Forlaget Aprostof.

Disorders in children illustrated by the dynamic interaction between neuropsychological and developmental psychological factors. Susan Hart and Cand. Psych. Ida Møller.
www.neuroaffect.dk/Artikler_pdf/kas2.pdf

Children from overprotective families, interestingly enough, are the ones who grow up more prone to narcissism, anxiety and depression.
http://www.abc.net.au/science/articles/2012/08/20/3570084.htm

Cortisol affects children's brains. Sue Gerhart (2004): *Why Love Matters: How affection shapes a baby's brain. (*p. 264), Routledge.

Social and emotional skills can be learned just like any other skill. They must be made visible in words and actions, supported and recognized to be developed. One of the most important skills a child learns through childhood is to relate to others. Step by Step is a complete program designed to prevent bullying and violence, promote empathy and develop the child's social skills. A child with social skills can master many skills. Step by Step is an educational, systematic and structured logically and practically applicable program to develop these competences: empathy, impulse control and problem solving.
The program is developed by CESEL. http://spf-nyheder.dk/download/om_cesel.pdf

CAT-kit.: www.cat-kit.com/?lan=en&area=catbox&page=catbox

The Mary Foundation. http://www.maryfonden.dk/en

The protégé effect. *Why teaching is the best way to learn.*
http://ideas.time.com/2011/11/30/the-protege-effect/

Studies show that there is a huge learning curve in helping others.
www.voresborn.dk/barn-3-8/psykologi-og-udvikling/4254-laer-dit-barn-at-vaere-god-mod-andre

We know that empathy is one of the single biggest factors in making successful leaders, entrepreneurs, managers and businesses (19). http://www.forbes.com/sites/ashoka/2013/05/30/why-empathy-is-the-force-that-moves-business-forward/

Empathic teenagers are shown to be more successful because they are more purpose driven than their more narcissistic counterparts. http://www.psychologytoday.com/blog/promoting-empathy-your-teen/201005/are-empathetic-teenagers-more-likely-be-intentionally-succes

.

Knud Ejler Løgstrup:
www.kristeligt-dagblad.dk/debat/fasthold-den-etiske-fodring-fortællinger-udvikler-børns-empati & www.kristeligt-dagblad.dk/liv-sjæl/i-begyndelsen-er-tilliden

Lisa is playing by the sea is taken from an example to illustrate empathy, limits and what to do.
Juul, Jesper (2008): *Din kompetente familie*; Forlaget Aprostof. http://www.family-lab.com/about/jesper-juul-articles/item/empati-3

Studies show that reading to your children markedly increases their empathy levels. *Exposure to Media and Theory-of-Mind Development in Preschoolers*. R. Mar, J. Tackett and C. Moore in Cognitive Development 2010: Vol. 25, pages 69–78.

Having fractured relationships has been proven to cause physical and psychological damage. http://www.psychologytoday.com/blog/our-empathic-nature/201205/forgiveness-when-and-why-do-we-forgive

Empathy and forgiveness activate the same region of the brain. Zheng Y, Wilkinson ID, Spence SA, Deakin JF, Tarrier N, Griffiths PD, Woodruff PW. *Investigating the functional anatomy of empathy and forgiveness*. Neuroreport 2001 Aug. Farrow TF1.

Meaningful friend and family relationships are the top factors in true happiness, well above having a lot of money. http://bigthink.com/users/talbenshahar

No Ultimatums

Some studies suggest that up to 90 percent of Americans still use spanking at some time as a form of discipline. http://www.scientificamerican.com/article/to-spank-or-not-to-spank/ Corporal punishment is still allowed in schools. That is, hitting students with a paddle or a cane for misbehaving. Although corporal punishment in schools has been banned in 31 states, it is still allowed in private schools in 50 states. http://en.wikipedia.org/wiki/School_corporal_punishment

(Non-Hispanic whites and American Indians) composed of 240 focus groups in 6 different cities across the US found that all of the groups claimed, at some time or another, to use physical punishment when necessary. Lubell KM, Lofton T, Singer HH. *Promoting Healthy Parenting Practices Across Cultural Groups*: A CDC Research Brief. Atlanta (GA): Centers for Disease Control and Prevention, National Center for Injury Prevention and Control, 2008.

What was even more striking were the differences across cultures in terms of when and where they spanked. Lubell KM, Lofton T, Singer HH. *Promoting Healthy Parenting Practices Across Cultural Groups*: A CDC Research Brief. Atlanta (GA): Centers for Disease Control and Prevention, National Center for Injury Prevention and Control, 2008.

There are four different parenting styles commonly identified in literature. www.education.com/reference/article/parenting-styles-2/ Baumrind, D. Current patterns of parental authority. *Developmental Psychology Monographs* (1971): 4 (1, Pt.2).

Diane Baumrind has studied the different ways in which parents raise their children. http://familieraadgiveren.webbyen.dk/vishjemmeside_privat.asp?mode=top_frame&id=1212356&side=&webside=8108302

Some of the challenges associated with authoritarian parenting are that being very controlling can make kids rebel. http://www.ahaparenting.com/parenting-tools/positive-discipline/strict-parenting http://www.ahaparenting.com/BlogRetrieve.aspx?PostID=17 9672&A=SearchResult&SearchID=2341008&ObjectID=179672&ObjectType=55

A recent analysis covering two decades' worth of research on the long-term effects of physical punishment on children concludes that spanking not only doesn't work, but can actually wreak havoc on kids' long-term development. Harriet L. MacMillan, MD, Michael H. Boyle, PhD, Maria Y.-Y. Wong, MSc, Eric K. Duku, MSc, Jan E. Fleming, MD, Christine A. Walsh, MSW. *Slapping and spanking in childhood and its association with lifetime prevalence of psychiatric disorders in a general population sample.* October 5, 1999 vol. 161 no. 7.

There's neuroimaging evidence that physical punishment may alter parts of the brain involved in performance on IQ tests. Tomoda A, Suzuki H, Rabi K, Sheu Y, Polcari A, Teicher MH. *Reduced prefrontal cortical gray matter volume in young adults exposed to harsh corporal punishment.* NeuroImage. (2009): 47(2):T66–T71.

Corporal punishment and substance abuse. There is data that spanking can affect areas of the brain involved in emotion and stress regulation. Afifi TO, Mota NP, Dasiewicz P, et al. *Physical punishment and mental disorders: results from a nationally representative US sample.* Pediatrics (2012): 130:184–92.

Case in point; one mother in the George Holden study hit her toddler after the toddler either hit or kicked her mother, saying, "This is to help you remember not to hit your mother." "The irony is just amazing," says Holden. http://healthland.time.com/2011/06/28/would-you-record-yourself-spanking-your-kids/
https://www.youtube.com/watch?v=N3iwOpy_PL8

Corporal punishment was gradually prohibited by law during the 20th century. The punishment of servants was prohibited in 1921 and in 1951 corporal punishment was abolished in

public schools in Copenhagen. The "Cane Circular" of 1967 finally put an end to any form of physical punishment in Danish schools. The right of parents to chastise their own children remained unchallenged. After the abolition of corporal punishment, violence against children became punishable under the Penal Code to the same extent as violence against others.
http://da.wikipedia.org/wiki/Revselsesret
And now more than 32 countries—much of Europe, Costa Rica, Israel, Tunisia and Kenya—have similar laws. http://en.wikipedia.org/wiki/Corporal_punishment_in_the_home

Studies show children of authoritative parents are more likely to become self-reliant, socially accepted, academically successful and well-behaved. They are less likely to report depression or anxiety, and are less likely to engage in antisocial behavior like delinquency and drug use. Fletcher A, Steinberg L, and Sellers E. *Adolescents' well-being as a function of perceived inter-parent inconsistency*. Journal of Marriage and the Family (1999): 61: 300-310. Wener, E. E. & Smith, R. S. (1982): *Vulnerable but invincible*: *A study of resilient children*. New York: McGraw-Hill.

Research suggests that having even one authoritative parent can make a huge difference. Fletcher A, Steinberg L, and Sellers E. *Adolescents' well-being as a function of perceived inter-parent inconsistency*. Journal of Marriage and the Family (1999): 61: 300-310.

They are also more attuned to their parents and less influenced by their peers.
Bednar, D.E. & Fisher, T.D. *Peer referencing in adolescent decision making as a function of perceived parenting style.* Adolescence (2003): 38, 607-621.

Involving all students in getting the class to act as a socially responsible community is a process that begins in nursery school and persists when pupils leave school. This work contributes to the prevention of disorder and is also important in terms of making school bullying-free.
The school should be aware that recess is an area where children learn through play and to learn to play. This is where they must learn the need for fair play.
Danmarks Lærerforening, July 2009. www.dlf.org/media/97473/UroISkolen2.pdf

Ball cushion. www.protac.dk/ball_cushion.aspx?ID=120

Photos of balance sheets and pillow balloon.
www.podconsult.dk/inklusiononline/flyers/sidderedskaber%202.pdf

Cuddling gizmos and cots. www.familierum.dk/forside/category/dimse

Running laps in schoolyards.
Today, we know that physical activity is essential for the development of children's health, motor and cognitive skills, social skills and personal identity. Since it is also a universal experience of many teachers that many children experience high motivation of learning through movement, there is good reason to implement motion as a regular part of everyday teaching. Therefore, the Health Department, Public Health Copenhagen and Children and Youth Administration, Center for Children and Youth, initiated a collaboration to develop inspirational material to come up with concrete instructions and provide inspiration for how teachers in subjects such as Danish, mathematics, English, German and history may involve movement and physical activity as a component of academic instruction. This material is called: *Exercise in class—a project of Learning for All*. www.laengelevekbh.kk.dk/Sundhed/~/media/folkesundhed/Files/BoernOgUnge/MotionIKlassen.ashx

Differentiate.
www.uvm.dk/Den-nye-folkeskole/Udvikling-af-undervisning-og-laering/Inklusion-og-undervisningsdifferentiering
www.inklusionsudvikling.dk/Vores-fire-fokusomraader/Inkluderende-laeringsfaellesskab/Laeringsmiljoeer/Undervisningsdifferentiering-saa-alle-elever-udfordres-og-motiveres

Children's development stages.
Jean Piaget (August 9, 1896 in Neuchatel—September 16, 1980) was a Swiss psychologist who is known for his studies of thought processes in children. His findings have had a significant influence on contemporary teaching methods. Piaget considered the child's per-

ception as unstable, distorted and filled with illusions and learning processes, or growing up, as a gradual approximation to a more orderly and systematic world of experience that helps the child to adapt to his or her environment. He divides this stage theory into the following: Senso-motor stage: 0-2 years old, pre-operational phase 2-6 years, concrete-operational phase 6-12 years and abstract-operational stage 12+. www.leksikon.org/art. php?n=2026

Erik Erikson (1902-1994) was a German-American psychoanalyst and developmental psychologist. Personality is shaped much more by the child´s relationship with his/her parents than by instincts and sexuality, and it develops through a series of psychosocial stages that go from infancy to old age.
Ewen, Robert B. (2003): *An Introduction to Theories of Personality*. Sixth Edition. Lawrence Erlbaum Associates, Inc.

Extra Resources and Further Inspiration

Both for the teachers' and students' own sake, students should learn appropriate behavior with different adults. According to the Education Act (Folkeskoleloven) involving the teacher as far as possible the students in planning and organizing the teaching, and the school will work with parents on teaching.
www.uvm.dk/Uddannelser/Folkeskolen/Love-og-regler-for-folkeskolen

Agency points to the relationship to become an actor in one's own life in the importance of creating opportunities to trade and make their own choices. Olsen, Thorkild (2009) contribution to the newspaper Venire.

Togetherness and Hygge

Research shows that one of the top predictors of well-being and happiness is quality time with friends and family. http://time.com/14296/6-secrets-you-can-learn-from-the-happiest-people-on-earth/, http://bigthink.com/users/talbenshahar

Jeppe Trolle Linnet from the Department of Marketing and Management at the Syddansk University is one of the few people in the world who has specialized in hygge. "Hygge is not just fun. Hygge is what we identify us with. Hygge is what the coming of Christmas is centered on. To hygge with other people, get the things away that distract one from the moment," he says. www.rustonline.dk/2013/12/12/hygge-i-et-seriost-lys/

Geert Hofstede, a world-renowned cultural psychologist, concluded in a very famous study about cultural differences that America had the highest level of individualism in the world. Geert Hofstede (2001): *Culture's Consequences: Comparing Values, Behaviors, Institutions and Organizations Across Nations*. 2nd Edition, Thousand Oaks CA: Sage Publications, Geert Hofstede (1997): *Cultures and Organizations: Software of the Mind*. 1st edition, McGraw-Hill USA.

"When you replace the "I" for the "We" even illness becomes wellness." Sushan R Sharma. http://www.searchquotes.com/quotes/author/Sushan_R_Sharma/5/

A fable that illustrates substituting the "I" for the "we" and its effects. http://en.wikipedia.org/wiki/Allegory_of_the_long_spoons

Teamwork in Denmark. "Foreningsliv" TNS Gallup is behind the DUF (2014). www.duf.dk

Singing and hygge. http://www.telegraph.co.uk/health/healthnews/10496056/Choir-singing-boosts-your-mental-health.html

Researchers at Brigham Young University and the University of North Carolina at Chapel Hill pooled data from 148 studies on health outcomes and their correlation to social relationships. Holt-Lunstad J, Smith TB, Layton JB (2010): *Social Relationships and Mortality Risk: A Meta-analytic Review*. PLoS Med 7(7): e1000316. doi:10.1371/journal. pmed.1000316.

In another famous experiment on health and social ties, Sheldon College at Carnegie Mellon University exposed hundreds of healthy volunteers to the common cold virus. Cohen, S., Doyle, W. J., Turner, R. B., Alper, C. M., & Skoner, D. P. *Sociability and susceptibility to the common cold*. Psychological Science (2003): 14, 389-395.

A research group in Chicago studied this affect and confirms it. Social support does, in fact, help manage stress. Pressman, S. D., Cohen, S., Miller, G.E., Barkin, A., Rabin, B. S., Treanor, J. J. *Loneliness, Social Network Size and Immune Response to Influenza Vaccination in College Freshmen*, Health Psychology (2005).

Research shows that people who try to be tough in a tragedy will suffer for a much longer period than those who share their emotions and are vulnerable with others. http://bigthink.com/users/talbenshahar

Yet, research shows that the reaction new mothers often have to this difficult period is to reduce the amount of social support rather than increase it. Joseph, S., Dalgleish, T., Thrasher, S. & Yule, W. *Crisis support and emotional reactions following trauma*. Crisis Intervention & Time-Limited Treatment (1995): 1(3), 203-208.

Support from friends, family members and parent groups has been clearly proven to help new mothers deal better with stress and thereby making them able to see their children in a more positive light. Andersen, P. A. & Telleen, S. L. *The relationship between social support and maternal behaviors and attitudes: A meta-analytic review*. American Journal of Community Psychology (1992): 20(6), 753-774.

Extra Resources and Further Inspiration

This movie tells about the importance of togetherness/friends and support and is the fundament of "outsider witness" that we use in narrative therapy.

http://www.amazon.com/Number-Our-Days-Triumph-Continuity/dp/0671254308

About Barbara Myerhoff. http://www.indiana.edu/~wanthro/theory_pages/Myerhoff.htm

Danes want to help. According to the most comprehensive inventory of the global charity, Charities Aid Foundation's World Giving Index, Denmark was in seventh place in 2012, measured by the proportion of the population who donate to charity. Approximately 70 percent of Danes donate money each year to charity.

www.information.dk/455623

Singing. www.kristeligt-dagblad.dk/historie/den-danske-sang-er-enstemmig-og-hjemmestrikket www.kristeligt-dagblad.dk/danmark/2014-06-21/den-danske-sangskat-er-årtiets-bog-succes

INDEX